TEACHING DISCIPLINARY LITERACY

TEACHING DISCIPLINARY LITERACY

USING VIDEO RECORDS OF PRACTICE TO IMPROVE SECONDARY TEACHER PREPARATION

Charles W. Peters, Deanna Birdyshaw,
and Amy Bacevich

Foreword by Karen Wixson

TEACHERS COLLEGE PRESS

TEACHERS COLLEGE | COLUMBIA UNIVERSITY

NEW YORK AND LONDON

Published by Teachers College Press, 1234 Amsterdam Avenue, New York, NY 10027

Cover design by Holly Grundon / BHG Graphic Design

Library of Congress Cataloging-in-Publication Data

Names: Peters, Charles W., 1944- | Birdyshaw, Deanna. | Bacevich, Amy.
Title: Disciplinary literacy : using video records of practice to improve secondary teacher
    preparation / Charles W. Peters, Deanna Birdyshaw, Amy Bacevich.
Description: New York, NY : Teachers College Press, 2016. | Includes bibliographical
    references and index.
Identifiers: LCCN 2016004704 (print) | LCCN 2016007266 (ebook)
ISBN 9780807757673 (pbk. : alk. paper)
ISBN 9780807773574 (ebook)
Subjects: LCSH: Audio-visual education. | Video recordings. | Teachers—Training of.
Classification: LCC LB1043 .P48 2016 (print) | LCC LB1043 (ebook) | DDC
    373.133/5dc23
LC record available at http://lccn.loc.gov/2016004704

ISBN 978-0-8077-5767-3 (paper)
ISBN 978-0-8077-7357-4 (ebook)

Printed on acid-free paper
Manufactured in the United States of America

23 22 21 20 19 18 17 16   8 7 6 5 4 3 2 1

In part this book is dedicated to my brother, Dave, who died during the last phases of its completion. He was a consummate educator whose indomitable zest for knowledge, engagement with ideas, and dedication and devotion to teaching influenced thousands of his students. The education profession has lost one of its jewels.—CWP

Without the support of family and friends, this book would not have been finished. Without the intellectual guidance of my colleagues and students, this book could not have been written. Thank you. —DB

With gratitude for my fellow teacher educators, who inspire me to try to do the work better for the right reasons. —AB

Contents

Foreword

I readily agreed to write this Foreword because I always learn something when considering the ideas put forward by the authors of this book. I first met and collaborated with Charlie and Deanna in the early 1980s when they were still working in K–12 education. We met as a result of our mutual involvement with the Michigan Reading Association and the Michigan Department of Education in developing new state reading tests and, somewhat later, state standards in ELA. This collaboration resulted in new approaches to reading assessment that are still in use today, most notably in the National Assessment of Educational Progress (NAEP) reading frameworks and assessments.

As the title suggests, this book is about using video records of practice in secondary teacher preparation. And, to be sure, an understanding of how to design and implement video records of practice is important, especially as accreditation and evaluation standards and assessments increasingly emphasize this approach to teacher preparation and assessment. However, you won't need to read very far to understand that this book is about so much more than the title suggests. Video records of practice are just one component of an entire system of secondary teacher preparation. In many ways, this book is a blueprint for the design and implementation of a secondary teacher preparation program aimed at developing a "strategic" teacher, which the authors define as one ". . . who is able to integrate pedagogical and disciplinary knowledge and practice in a skillful, adept manner; who knows *when, how,* and *why* to implement a core literacy practice; who demonstrates the ability to judge accurately the quality of the core practice; who analyzes and contextualizes decision-making; and who uses professional language explicitly, accurately, and confidently to describe his or her practice or the practice of others" (p. 38).

The integration of pedagogical and disciplinary knowledge and practice is at the heart of the vision of a strategic teacher presented in this book. As the Common Core State Standards (CCSS) and other College and Career Readiness (CCR) standards have been implemented across the country, they have renewed debates about content vs. skills/processes in curriculum and instruction. Some proponents of the new CCR standards advocate content over process, and others continue to view these standards as a new list of skills. Programs such as the one described here rightly address the development of skills and processes in the service of subject-area content—for both teachers and their students. This is a principle that the authors have written about and worked with for many years, and is part of the foundation for the program and practices they describe.

We often hear about the need for theory- and/or research-based practice in our schools and teacher preparation programs, and the field is constantly striving to develop programs and practices that reflect this need. Yet it is rare to find examples of programs such as the one described in this volume where theory and research related to foundational precepts, essential content, and design principles have been combined to inform a system of curriculum, instruction, and assessment in secondary teacher preparation (see Figure 2.1 on p. 15). Programs like this are, of necessity, always a work in progress. However, after 7 years of development, there is much to be learned from the experiences of the authors in refining the ideas and practices that comprise this program, including the manner in which video records are used to improve secondary teacher preparation. I recommend this volume to its readers as a terrific example of bringing to bear the current state of knowledge across relevant areas to address persistent issues in the development and assessment of programs designed for secondary teacher preparation.

—Karen Wixson
William E. Moran Distinguished Professor in Reading and Literacy,
University of North Carolina at Greensboro

Acknowledgments

The authors gratefully acknowledge all the interns in our teacher education program who allowed us to learn from their efforts at using video study. Learning the complex task of teaching is difficult and sometimes frustrating. These interns diligently took on this challenge while also graciously accommodating their instructors' efforts to understand and improve the practice of teacher education. We thank you for making this book possible.

Kim Alberts	Kevin Hankinson	R. J. Quiambao
Diane Aretz	Jessica Highfield	Tasha Rios
Rachel Baumgold	Jimmy Johnson	Paul Sandy
Hussein Beydoun	Muneer Khalid	Holly Shelton
Abby Boggs	Kyle Tecmire	Elijah Smith
Mary Braun	Anna Luchtefeld	Stephen Smith
Mindy Broderick	Rebeca Maxon	John Spisak
Carl Dixon	Alex Mendiola	Samantha Stemmer
Kelsey Ehnle	Naomi Miller	Lisa Sullivan
David Golden	Derek Mohr	Betsy Swigart
Kareem Hakim	Branden Prather	Samantha Wakefield

Part I

THEORETICAL FRAMEWORK FOR USING VIDEO STUDY TO TEACH CORE LITERACY PRACTICES

CHAPTER 1

The Importance of Video Records of Practice in Teacher Education

Developing Core Literacy Practices

Imagine a university multipurpose space. Three teaching interns in a secondary teacher preparation program are gathered in a brightly colored booth facing a large computer monitor. They are preparing to share video records of practice that represent their early teaching practice. Lynne, who is in her first month of student teaching at a local high school, begins to introduce her video, saying, "This is my world history class." She goes on to provide more background:

> Right now we're finishing up watching a movie called *Invisible Children*. It's a documentary that came out in 2005 about college-age students who went to Sudan to document the travesties going on. They found out about another issue in Uganda, kids being forced into being child soldiers. As a bigger theme of this class, we've gone through how individuals in the different movies that we've watched throughout history have been able to make a difference. . . . In this video they are supposed be having a substantive conversation. I wanted them to connect private research they'd done on Uganda to what is happening in the film. I started them in small groups to get them warmed up and then we attempted a whole-class substantive conversation.

Lynne also describes her "focus question," or the aspect of her teaching that she wants the group to discuss:

> My focus question is: What else could I have done to create more meaningful conversation by students in small groups? One of the things I've pulled out from our other video discussions is that when I was doing group discussions with the class, only about four or five people were talking. So in this situation I broke them out into small groups of four randomly wherein each person was supposed to talk—instead of just four or five people talking in the class, all 35 were talking for at least some point. But even with this, some people were just asking questions and looking for answers and I wanted them to

have discussions. They're almost adults. I feel like they should be able to talk about what they think and what they see and make connections.

Lynne taps the laptop's keys and a video begins playing. The group watches the video in silence, with each member jotting notes occasionally. After the video finishes playing, Raina indicates a specific time marker: "Starting at 5:18 is where I pulled out something relevant to this." Lynne sets the video to that time marker and replays a brief portion. Raina goes on:

> What you did there is, you were trying to reframe what they were doing—you described some of the things they could talk about in order to create discussion. And it seemed like you already knew that George had a good response to the idea that you had posed. So you called on him, knowing what he would say. I thought that was good because he was sort of like a plant. I guess a suggestion for stimulating more conversation in the whole class is to work one-on-one with a student while you were observing the group and kind of say like, "What did you do? How do you think your research relates to the movie?" After him telling you what he knows, you can call on him and have him repeat it to stimulate more discussion with the whole class. That's especially good to get kids who don't usually talk to talk.

Lynne then notes that she had created a graphic organizer template that students could use to prepare for the whole-class discussion. She wonders aloud how she could have used it more effectively to stimulate meaningful conversation. Bob responds:

> Your graphic organizer, like you said, is good in terms of your organizing information, but I think you need to include something that allows them to express an opinion. Like, is this argument valid? Does this research match what we're talking about regarding Uganda and the movie? What you're doing is, you're having them relate the movie and their research, which is higher order of thinking, right, because they're applying their knowledge. But then I think there needs to be another step where they sort of apply the knowledge into a deeper conversation.

The interns then discuss how the use of an overarching question might stimulate substantive conversation among the high school students:

Bob: A question like, given what you know about this topic and what you know from the movie, is being a child soldier necessarily bad? They can draw on their research on how kids in Uganda live. Maybe as a child soldier they're guaranteed to eat, right?
Raina: Maybe it's better than this other option of dying.

Bob: They're able to protect themselves because they're trained and they have weapons.

Lynne: So would I be providing this overarching question for the small-group work or would I use it when we start the whole-class discussion?

This vignette illustrates the kinds of video-based discussions of novices' own teaching that have become a central feature of our teacher education program. After 10 intensive years of studying and researching video-based discussions of teaching, we are convinced of the power of novices' study of "records of practice" as part of their teacher preparation. By records of practice, we mean documentation and artifacts drawn directly from teaching and used to support video discussions. Documentation includes authentic recordings of classroom interactions, particularly the video representations of teachers' work with students in classrooms that have become the central focus of our teacher education program. Artifacts include such materials as lesson plans and notes, student work, and curriculum materials—concrete items that are part of teachers' work in classrooms. This book articulates what we have learned through our efforts to incorporate the study of video records of practice, supplemented by relevant teaching artifacts, to support interns' learning of core literacy practices in a master of arts in education with secondary certification program.

The lessons we share here regarding implementation and pedagogy will, we hope, be useful to other teacher educators seeking to use video records of practice in an ongoing way to support novices' learning to teach disciplinary literacy. In the following sections, we provide the background for our work with video records of practice, describe the theoretical framework that shaped our efforts, and discuss the chapters that follow.

A TEACHER EDUCATION CURRICULUM
FOCUSED ON VIDEO RECORDS OF PRACTICE

Our work with records of practice is situated in larger efforts to reform the teacher education curriculum. The quality of teaching in pre-K–12 classrooms is a prominent issue in the education discourse, highlighted in part by research confirming that teachers are a critical factor in students' achievement (Rowan, Correnti, & Miller, 2002; Sanders & Rivers, 1996). As a result, teacher preparation programs have come under scrutiny and are often perceived as outdated and inadequate (Rich, 2014). In one instance of such criticism, commentator George Will (2006) argued that schools of education fail to address pre-K–12 students' true needs by focusing not on effective teaching skills and strategies, but on fuzzy aspects of teacher preparation such as "professional dispositions" and the development of "child-centered" philosophies. This focus on the teacher education curriculum—or lack thereof—is a regular complaint. The "confusing patchwork" of the teacher education curriculum (Levine, 2006) includes variable approaches (Hiebert, Morris, Berk, & Jansen, 2007), uncertain outcomes (Zeichner, 2006), and no shared language to describe its most important elements (Grossman & McDonald, 2008).

Several prominent teacher education researchers have positioned records of practice to play a key role in the reform of the teacher education curriculum (e.g., Ball & Cohen, 1999; Lampert & Ball, 1998; Stigler & Hiebert, 1997). Records of practice have multiple potential benefits for novices' learning to teach. They can represent multiple aspects of the work of teaching, from planning to instruction to assessment, and provide a common space for preservice teachers to jointly examine issues related to these aspects. At the same time, studying records can help novices develop the understanding that pre-K–12 teaching is a complex, multifaceted practice. The implementation of a strong teacher education curriculum focused on the use of records of practice engages novices in systematic study of the work of teaching, as opposed to approaching teaching in a piecemeal manner. Within a supportive instructional framework, records of practice can provide access to ways of doing teaching (ways of moving, speaking, organizing, and so on) as well as the "know-how"—the principles, judgments, and understanding—that is essential to teaching. As they engage in such study, novices can develop dispositions of professional inquiry that they can use throughout their teaching careers.

It should be noted that, among the many formats for records of practice, we focus primarily on videos of teaching and the artifacts related to their study. Video has characteristics that make it a powerful medium for records of practice. Videos can capture much of the complexity of instruction in the form of a "text" that can then be studied. In contrast with in-the-moment teaching, videos provide a lasting record; they can be collected and edited; and they enable certain kinds of interaction, including time to reflect, develop collegiality, and engage in fine-grained analysis (Sherin, 2004). Other records of practice, such as copies of lesson plans and student work, are also used in our program, but serve mainly to amplify and refine the ideas raised in video-based discussions. Our premise, which will be elaborated in this book, is that videos of novices' own teaching are particularly powerful learning tools because they focus attention on the context (including knowledge of students, subject matter, and classroom resources) that informs teachers' decisions. In our experience, videos also served as a motivating factor for the teacher education interns, who were eager to share their practice with understanding colleagues and support their colleagues' learning from their own teaching.

Over the past 10 years, we have endeavored to use records of practice, and videos in particular, in a comprehensive way in our secondary teacher education program. We had two sets of goals for this endeavor. First, we set goals related to what we wanted interns to learn through the study of videos and other records of their own practice. Those goals included the following:

- To develop competence with teaching five core literacy practices that facilitate secondary students' learning of disciplinary content
- To analyze, evaluate, and practice teaching as complex relationships among significant disciplinary content, pedagogical decision-making, and students' responses to instruction for the purpose of improving student learning
- To engage in professional conversation for the purpose of facilitating critical reflection on practice
- To develop the dispositions and resources to carry the study of video and other records of practice into the first years of teaching

Second, we had goals for how we wanted to revise the teacher education program curriculum:

- To make interns' study of video and other records of practice an essential component of (not a supplement to) secondary teacher preparation
- To develop aligned assignments, protocols, and tools that make substantive use of video and other records of practice for interns' study of core literacy practices across teacher education courses
- To document and communicate interns' progress over time as they develop into strategic practitioners

This book tells the story of our progress toward these goals as we developed a thoughtful curriculum for using video records of practice to prepare teacher education interns to enter the workplace as competent beginning teachers in secondary content area classrooms. The content of this book addresses our refined understanding of how records of practice can be effectively conceptualized and used in an ongoing way to support novices' learning the work of teaching, and in particular, their ability to teach core literacy practices.

THEORETICAL FRAMEWORK

Our work builds upon three related lines of research that have significant implications for reforming the teacher education curriculum: (1) the building of a "practice-based" approach to teacher education, (2) the identification of core practices within the profession, and (3) the enactment of a theoretical framework that grounds the teacher education curriculum in professional practice.

First, our work with video records of practice was guided by a conviction that novice teachers' learning should be "practice-based." This notion can be traced to Ball and Cohen's (1999) call for making teaching itself the focus of professional study—a move that "would require teachers [to] become serious learners in and around their practice" (p. 4). To realize Ball and Cohen's vision for teacher

education, and to understand the role of video records of practice within that vision, requires two elements: a conception of teaching as a practice and an understanding of how practice can be accessed, studied, and enacted by novices.

The literature on teaching and teacher education is replete with efforts to conceptualize the work of teaching. Research on microteaching in the 1960s and 1970s,
for example, was based on a behavioral view of teaching—the idea that teaching
was fundamentally a set of skills that were effective regardless of context, and that
novices could acquire these skills through modeling and practice (see, for example,
Gage, 1968). In the 1980s and 1990s, a cognitive perspective on teaching emerged;
this view addressed, for example, the near-constant decisions involved in teaching,
as teachers encounter dilemmas in their efforts to manage variation, interaction,
and complexity to enable student learning (Lampert, 1985). These efforts brought
to light teachers' knowledge and reasoning, which is often tacit, highly contextu-
alized, and difficult to observe and define (Leinhardt, 1989). Later, Nel Noddings
(2003) characterized teaching as a "relational" practice; that is, teachers' work depends on sustaining productive relationships with students in order to engage them
with the subject matter under study. These perspectives, among many others, represent efforts to make teaching comprehensible and learnable, and have shaped the
teacher education curriculum in variable ways over the years.

Recently, scholars in the fields of teaching and teacher education have pulled
together these behavioral, cognitive, and relational aspects of teaching to develop a comprehensive conception of teaching as a *practice*. In lay terms, the word
practice implies action—it might be considered a synonym for *things that we do*.
However, enacting a practice involves more than mere muscular coordination,
such as that involved in hitting a golf ball correctly or cutting seconds off a down-
hill ski run. In education, we "practice" with the goal of guiding others to think
or act differently—for example, we seek to focus students' attention on important
disciplinary content, to improve students' reading and writing skills, or to prepare
students for an upcoming test. Achieving the goal involves acting with "specialized
knowledge and practical wisdom . . . to bring about a specific change of state in
behavior or solve a problem" (Namubiru, 2007, pp. 45–46). We use knowledge
and skill to make judgments that inform the action—"the orchestration of understanding, skill, relationship, and identity to accomplish particular activities with
others in specific environments" (Grossman, Compton, Igra, Ronfeldt, Shahan,
& Williamson, 2009, p. 2059). A focus on practice foregrounds teaching as active
work—involving ways of speaking, moving, organizing, and so on—that is intertwined with ways of thinking, knowing, and relating. Rather than reading about
or imagining what teaching would be like, novices have carefully designed opportunities to investigate and enact the real thing. Advocates of a practice-based curriculum assert that an unwavering focus on teaching can enable novices to learn to
do the active work in tandem with the know-how (the principles, judgments, and
understanding) that drives teachers' decisions to act (Lampert & Graziani, 2009).
Video records of practice, as rich representations of teaching, can be key tools
within a practice-based teacher education curriculum. However, the effectiveness

of video records of practice (as with any instructional resource) depends on how they are conceptualized and used, which points toward the second and third lines of research that informed our work—the identification of core practices and the enactment of a curricular framework based in professional practice.

A second line of research focuses on identifying *core practices* (Grossman, Hammerness, & McDonald, 2009; Grossman & Shahan, 2005). Core practices are the recognizable routines, approaches, or activities that form the foundation of effective teaching. In Grossman, Hammerness, and McDonald's (2009) terms, core practices occur with high frequency in teaching, are used across various curricula, and are research-based. They note that as a central feature of the teacher education curriculum, core practices are learnable by novices and allow them to learn about both students and teaching. For our purposes, we identified five core literacy practices that will be elaborated later in this book: graphic organizers, questioning techniques, text-based learning, thinking routines, and concept attainment.

The notion of core practices goes hand in hand with the concept of *high leverage practice,* which encompasses characteristics of core teaching practices that significantly increase the likelihood that teaching will achieve the goals of instruction and result in students demonstrating the desired learning outcomes. (The concept of high leverage practice is further elaborated in Chapter 3.) Drawing on the work of Ball and Forzani (2010), we introduced interns to the concept of and language related to high leverage practice. It became a lens for examining, assessing, and improving their teaching of core literacy practices as represented in videos and other records of practice.

The third line of research that informed our work with video records of practice was the development of a framework that could guide the transformation of teacher education—one that was research-based, practice-based, and consistent with ideas about core practices. Specifically, we drew upon the framework articulated by Pam Grossman and colleagues (Grossman, Compton, Igra, Ronfeldt, Shahan, & Williamson, 2009). The authors sought to inform the kinds of activities that might be central to a practice-based teacher education curriculum based on their study of professional preparation in three domains: clergy, clinical psychology, and teaching. They note that these three professions, though they differ significantly, share key characteristics: All are relational, meaning they depend on productive interaction between the professional and the client, and all require complex work in uncertain conditions.

The framework proposed by Grossman, Compton et al. has three parts. First, the authors describe *representation*—the ways practitioners' work is made visible to those studying it. Second, they describe *decomposition,* or ways practice is broken down into parts so that novices can see, discuss, and enact the work in manageable ways. Finally, they describe *approximations,* or simplified opportunities to engage in practice that are very similar to the real thing, which provide opportunity for specific feedback from instructors. In an effort to make the framework more complete, Moss (2011) added a fourth category: "conceptions of quality," which refers to *documentation* based on specific criteria that define effective practice and how those criteria should be used to document the quality of learning that occurs in a variety of contexts. Taken together, all four elements of what we call the "enhanced framework" (representation, decomposition, approximations, and documentation of quality) are critical to grounding teacher preparation in the practice of professionals. These four elements combine to establish a framework that can be used to guide decisions about what the curriculum of teacher education should entail. Notably, the four elements of the enhanced framework are not meant to be considered discretely. They are overlapping constructs that might enable a novice to recognize, study, and engage in essential elements of the work while gaining understanding of the complex whole.

This enhanced framework guided our use of video records of practice. These representations of teaching focused on the interns' approximation of core practices in a highly scaffolded instructional setting. Each video discussion focused on breaking down (decomposing) core literacy practices into their constituent parts, so that the complex work of teaching became "visible" to the teacher education students. Because the videos were captured and studied over time, both instructors and interns were able to observe and document their progress with particular aspects of teaching practice.

ORGANIZATION OF THE BOOK

This book represents our efforts to articulate what we have learned through 10 intensive years of using records of practice, and especially videos of novices' own teaching, as a central feature of our teacher education curriculum. We will illustrate how individuals, resources, and program history shaped our use of video records of practice. With that goal, this book is more than a "how-to" guide; however, we will address our practical experiences with developing a conceptual framework, creating assignments and instructional tools, and supporting our interns' efforts to study their teaching. We believe video records of practice are essential to novices' learning within a practice-based teacher education curriculum, and we hope our experiences may be informative to others seeking to develop practice-based programs.

The book is divided into two Parts. Part I lays the groundwork for understanding the use of video records of practice in teacher education, building on the argument begun in this chapter for the importance of records of practice within a practice-based curriculum. Chapter 2 describes our teacher education program structure, emphasizing a curriculum decision-making model derived from particular design principles, foundational precepts, and strong content. Chapter 3 more fully describes the concept of "high leverage practice" and elaborates on the five core literacy practices that were the focus of our interns' video study. Chapter 4 discusses how we applied the enhanced framework to document growth by developing a trajectory that was used to authenticate the quality of work of our interns.

Part II is practical. In Chapter 5, we describe two video-based assignments and the design questions we used to guide their development. In Chapter 6, we describe the first part of the Instructional Video Assignment in detail, focusing on the planning of the lesson and preparation of the video. We also describe interns' use of the characteristics of high leverage practice as an analytical lens for video-based study. Chapter 7 continues describing the Instructional Video Assignment, focusing on how to engage novices in substantive conversation about the quality of core literacy practices depicted in videos and complementary teaching artifacts. In Chapter 8 we turn to another important aspect of using video study as we discuss the value of critical reflection in transforming practice. Throughout Part II, we provide examples of interns' records of practice and reflections, sample assignment guidelines and rubrics, and vignettes from video discussion groups. We conclude in Chapter 9 by describing several lessons learned: about creating effective structures for learning with video records of practice, the importance of documenting intern progress, and the qualities that enhance coherence in a practice-based program in which video records of practice play a key role.

CHAPTER 2

Developing a Practice-Based Teacher Education Curriculum That Supports Video Study

Our teacher education program is similar to most in that we frequently encounter new research, promising practices, and the desire to incorporate new ideas into our teaching. This was certainly the situation when we added the use of video records of practice to our course structure and content. We found ourselves grappling with several questions: How will we make the significant curricular changes required in order to use video records of practice in the context of a well-established program? How can we ensure that the curricular changes are significant and worthwhile? How can we ascertain whether the curricular changes are coherent within and across courses? What criteria will we use to assess whether the changes are pro-ductive? The answers to questions such as these are certainly not simple, but they are far less problematic when grounded in foundational precepts and principles. Our programmatic decisions are guided by the conviction that teacher education students' learning should be "practice-based." This means teaching is understood as a *practice*—active work that is intertwined with ways of thinking, knowing, and relating—that is best taught through the use of core practices and directed by a research-based framework. Video records of practice, then, are framed as tools to make the practice of teaching accessible and studyable.

In this chapter, we briefly describe the context in which video records of practice were collected, shared, and studied. We explain the process we used to identify, incorporate, and implement new content as a result of the use of video records. We then describe a theoretically and pedagogically consistent approach to curricular decision-making that we used to incorporate the use of video records of practice into the program. We aligned the structure and content of program courses with precepts, principles, and design features that reflect the importance of a practice-based curriculum.

THE PROGRAM

Our teacher education program is an intensive, year-long, field-based program that has existed for over 25 years. "Interns" (which is what we call program participants) are required to take 40 graduate credit hours applied toward secondary school certification and a master of arts degree. The number of interns varies each year, but usually includes 40–50 individuals seeking certification in one of several disciplines: English, mathematics, science, social studies, or world languages. The program is accredited by the Michigan State Department of Education with reciprocity in nearly all other state certification programs. At the time this book was written, our program was ranked second in the nation by the *U.S. News and World Report* graduate school of education rankings (*U.S. News & World Report*, 2014).

Several features of the teacher education program are particularly supportive of our use of videos within a practice-based approach. The first is a year-long field placement—that is, interns work in a single classroom setting starting when the pre-K–12 school year begins in the fall and continuing until their mentor teachers check out of school for summer break. Interns have access to the tasks and routines of a full school year in a consistent setting, meaning that their field experience is closely aligned with the real work of teaching. They experience all the phases of a school year (opening days, professional development days, school open houses, parent–teacher conferences, midterm exams, final exams, closing day routines). They are able to study their students' development across the school year. By becoming part of the school community for a full year, with increasing responsibility for tasks, routines, and activities within that context, the interns are able to develop a strong sense of professionalism: They gain competence and confidence in the practice of teaching with a commitment to the particular school and students.

Peer networking is a second key feature. A major program goal is to help interns understand the importance of collegial relationships and in particular the benefits of collegial conversation. From the beginning of the program, interns are organized according to a cohort model (peer groupings) that assumes several configurations during the year. The first cohort configuration divides interns into two heterogeneous groups based on age, experience, gender, and disciplinary majors. Interns in these cohorts take the majority of their teacher education classes together, meaning that instruction occurs in classes of around 25 people. Interns can develop strong collegial connections with this subset of classmates. It also enables small-group discussions among interns who are preparing to teach in different disciplines.

A second configuration groups interns in five disciplinary cohorts (English, mathematics, science, social studies, and world languages). The disciplinary cohorts meet regularly throughout the year to study disciplinary pedagogy and share video records of practice. The size of the disciplinary cohorts varies from 5 to 20 members depending on the number of interns seeking certification in each discipline. Disciplinary cohorts are occasionally divided into even smaller cohorts based on student teaching placements (for example, urban or suburban communities, middle school or high school). Placing interns in cohorts establishes participation structures that encourage the high level social interaction that forms the foundation of our secondary teacher education program. The various cohort configurations enable different kinds of conversations around video records of practice.

One more program feature is perhaps most important for our purposes in this book: the explicit emphasis on using records of practice (and especially videos of teaching) to study and demonstrate competency in effective teaching. Throughout the program, interns collect and analyze videos of their teaching to illustrate their understanding of the standards and benchmarks that guide the program (see Appendix A). When they begin the program in the summer term, interns encounter core literacy practices (graphic organizers, questioning techniques, text-based learning, thinking routines, and concept attainment) using videos of veteran and novice teachers to unpack the teaching moves that are depicted. With modeling and support by faculty, interns begin to use the standards and benchmarks for effective teaching as well as the characteristics of high leverage practice to guide their analysis of video records of practice. During the fall and winter terms, interns record their own efforts to use core literacy practices. They engage in conversations with their peers about their growing proficiency, addressing how well they approximate the characteristics described in the standards and benchmarks and elements of high leverage practice. In the spring term, interns enroll in a seminar designed to support them as they write their master's thesis, an e-Portfolio that includes videos and other records of their own practice to illustrate the interns' growth over the year and their competency in teaching.

Interns work on two key video-based assignments: the Instructional Video Assignment and the Reflective Writing Task. Each assignment is designed to help interns represent the work of teaching, decompose it, and evaluate its quality as indicated by the enhanced framework (see below and Chapter 1 for elaboration on the enhanced framework). Both assignments are ongoing, meaning the interns work on each assignment over the course of the year-long program. The assignments require that the interns plan, teach, and then share video records of practice that incorporate use of core literacy practices. These assignments are elaborated and illustrated in later chapters.

Given the intensity of the program and the complexity of learning to teach, it is essential that interns recognize the connections between and among the courses they take, the assignments that they complete, and their experience in the field. The year-long placement, use of peer networking, and emphasis on video records of practice are features that provide coherence and cohesion, as does our continuous curriculum development. Next, we describe how we use a curriculum decision-making process to maximize interns' learning and the effectiveness of our curriculum.

CURRICULAR DECISION-MAKING

As teacher educators, many of us have been involved in conversations about the content of the courses we teach. Colleagues encounter new ideas in journal articles, books, or conference presentations and suggest changes to the program that have implications for course content. Such conversations can have a transformative effect, especially when the program is guided by clear understandings of how those decisions are reached. What follows is a description of the curriculum decision-making model we use to modify the curriculum (as we did with the incorporation of video records of practice) of the teacher education program in a manner that is theoretically sound, derived from high quality research, and filtered through program themes, beliefs, precepts, and principles (see Figure 2.1).

When we make important curricular decisions, we examine our design principles, foundational precepts, and strong program content to make sure there is a robust fit, both conceptually and theoretically (Peters & Kenney, 2003). There are three major components of our process. First, any new additions must adhere to our design principles: Content and courses must be coherent, cohesive, and aligned, based on sound research and pedagogy, and enacted with rigor. Second, we use foundational precepts to ensure that potential new content or courses are consistent with our vision for teacher education as practice-based, demonstrate

Figure 2.1. Curriculum Decision-Making Model

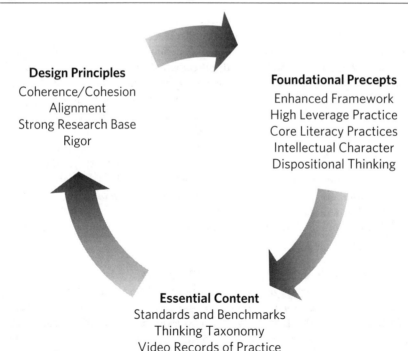

Design Principles
Coherence/Cohesion
Alignment
Strong Research Base
Rigor

Foundational Precepts
Enhanced Framework
High Leverage Practice
Core Literacy Practices
Intellectual Character
Dispositional Thinking

Essential Content
Standards and Benchmarks
Thinking Taxonomy
Video Records of Practice

intellectual character (Ritchhart, 2004, 2015), and are grounded in characteristics of high leverage practice (Ball & Forzani, 2010/2011). Third, the content must be strong, significant and worthwhile, clear and explicit, based on a strong cognitive foundation (Anderson & Krathwohl, 2001), and able to be studied with video and other records of practice. We use a set of standards and benchmarks that are based on several sources (Peters & Kenney, 2004): INTASC standards (Council of Chief State School Officers, 1992), the Stanford University Teacher Education Program (2002–2003), and the work of Charlotte Danielson (2007).

As Figure 2.1 suggests, the curriculum decision-making model is a process that can begin with consideration of any of the three components, depending on the nature of the decision being made. Therefore, it is not linear, but rather inter-active and recursive. The confluence of these three components provides a way of conceptualizing a curriculum for learning to teach in ways that will achieve im-portant instructional goals and result in interns demonstrating the desired learn-ing outcomes. What follows is a more detailed description of each component of our curriculum decision-making model.

Design Principles

One consideration in the curriculum decision-making model is a set of design principles that help ensure that the teacher education program is coherent and cohesive, guided by a strong theoretical foundation, and enacted with rigor. These have proven particularly important for systematically resolving differences related to curricular decisions; when there is disagreement or multiple options, our facul-ty can use the principles as a way to judge the appropriateness of potential chang-es to the curriculum. We use four principles on a consistent basis: (1) program courses, content, and assignments must be coherent and cohesive, demonstrating logical consistency in their arrangement and sequence; (2) content within a course and the attendant assignments must be aligned to demonstrate meaningful agree-ment among the parts and configured to demonstrate uniformity; (3) the courses in the program must have a strong theoretical and research foundation; and (4) the program must require interns to demonstrate competence in essential dimensions of successful teaching before they take full responsibility in the classroom, which means a commitment to rigor. Each principle is explained in more detail in the following section.

Coherence, Cohesion, and Alignment. The field of teacher education is chal-lenged by a traditionally fragmented curriculum that frequently leaves preservice novices underprepared for the realities of the classroom (American Federation of Teachers, 2000, 2012; Levine, 2006). The design principles of coherence and cohesion, which are macro-level organizational considerations, lead to the config-uration of courses and content in ways that provide stability and a holistic sense to the program's organizational structure. Our focus on coherence and cohesion helped us examine the arrangement and consistency of perspectives, concepts, and theories in courses across the program. The program's emphasis on core literacy practices is one example of a rich concept that is threaded throughout the program. The interns first encounter the concept in their summer coursework, when they begin to study how effective teachers represent knowledge and information. First, interns study the use of a graphic organizer in videos of experienced teachers' teaching. As the year progresses, interns continue to work on using a variety of techniques for representing knowledge and information, while also studying other core literacy practices (questioning techniques, text-based learning, thinking routines, and concept attainment) in a similarly systematic way involving a cycle of observation, practice, and feedback. As they gain proficiency with specific practices, the interns also develop a more complex concept of core practices as recognizable routines, approaches, or activities that form the foundation of effective teaching reflected in a practice-based curriculum. When courses are organized in a reasoned manner around a set of well-defined perspectives, concepts, and especially practices, interns are more likely to experience a coherent professional program that successfully prepares them for teaching.

Alignment and collaboration work in conjunction with coherence and cohesion. Alignment has both macro- and micro-level organizational functions, pulling together ideas related to content and assignments both within and across courses so that related parts fit together. For example, interns complete an e-Portfolio that documents their growth relative to their developing teaching practice across the 12 months of the program. A number of courses aligned their assignments to support interns' ongoing organization of artifacts from and reflections on their teaching across the program year. The process of alignment creates structures to facilitate better collaboration among course instructors as they seek to support interns' experience of a coherent teacher education program. Without such a commitment, a fragmented system prevails and interns' capacity to practice is uneven at best. Thus, through the process of alignment, we are able to achieve coherence and cohesion: Aligned assignments provide interns with opportunities to pull together concepts and ideas that cut across the program, thus allowing them to deepen their understanding of core literacy practices. Aligning involves collaboration, so assignments and course content create a coherent system where interns continuously grow—starting before they enter a classroom and through the end of the program.

Strong Theoretical and Research Foundation. At each decision point along the way, we ask: Do the practices, content, and methods that we embed within the program and courses have a strong theoretical and research foundation? This principle applies to the larger constructs of the program (the enhanced framework) as well as to the core literacy practices that are the focus of interns' work with video records of practice. For example, one of the four components of the enhanced framework is approximation, meaning that interns need multiple opportunities to rehearse a core practice under the supervision of an instructor or mentor teacher who gives them specific feedback designed to help them improve their practice.

Rigor. Just as in professions widely recognized for having a set of rigorous professional standards, such as law or medicine, teaching must have standards for entry into the profession. Albert Shanker (1996) wrote:

> To be considered a true profession, an occupation must: have a distinct body of knowledge—acknowledged by practitioner and consumer alike—that undergirds the profession and forms the basis of delivering high quality services to clients; define for itself the nature of training required of those who wish to enter the field; require rigorous training to acquire the knowledge and skills necessary to practice the profession; control the standards for entry into the profession; have its practitioners be a major voice in determining working conditions; have its practitioners exercise independent judgment about client needs to ensure those needs are met; evaluate the performance of practitioners and remove from the profession those whose performance fall below standards; require that practitioners continue to learn about advances in the field; induct its members into the profession in a systematic and rigorous fashion; and have the respect of the larger society. (p. 221)

The bottom line is that we must be concerned with rigor, and likewise with evidence of interns' development of strategic practice. Interns must demonstrate competence in essential dimensions of successful teaching before being allowed to take full responsibility in the classroom. In our effort to develop strategic practitioners, we have become acutely aware, as did Moss (2011), of the need to document individual growth. Without regard for the quality of interns' work as it develops over time, as depicted through representation, decomposition, and approximation (Grossman, Compton et al., 2009), teacher preparation lacks a quality control component. Thus, Moss (2011) argues for the importance of addressing the concept of quality, which could then trace novices' learning opportunities over time. She concluded:

> Even instructional practices that appeared quite similar when described through the lenses of approximations, decomposition, and representations looked quite different when conceptions of quality and learning opportunities and assessments were traced over time. Representing these "learning trajectories"—which entail an understanding of the evolving dialectical relationships between learning opportunities and (at least intended) learning outcomes—seems essential to understanding and learning from the teaching practice. (p. 2878)

In our experience, interns often have a "checklist" mentality about their assignments. They perceive each assignment within each course as a separate effort, rather than experiencing a trajectory of learning to teach. As a result, quality turns out to be relative: It is connected to grades received on individual assignments or in individual courses. The concept of quality must include documentation that is sensitive to capturing growth over time to counteract this checklist mentality. The use of videos and other records of practice across the 1-year program is a means of assessing growth (formally and informally by faculty and self-assessment by in-terns) within a broader concept of what constitutes effective teaching. (For a more detailed description of documenting growth over time, see Chapter 4.)

Foundational Precepts

Design principles are a broad lens for making curricular decisions, but their application still leaves a vast pool of potential content that might be addressed within the teacher education program. We began with a general notion that our curriculum should be practice-based. We knew we wanted a curriculum that enabled interns' proficiency with a number of core literacy practices. The teacher education program's foundational precepts, a second consideration in our curriculum decision-making model, provide a careful, deliberate means of selecting content and designing tasks and activities that are practice-based. The precepts are: (1) the enhanced framework, (2) core literacy practices and high leverage practice, and (3) intellectual character and dispositional thinking.

Enhanced Framework. The enhanced framework (Grossman, Compton et al., 2009; Moss, 2011) is a key foundational precept because it helps define practice-based teacher preparation. The enhanced framework encompasses four elements: (1) representation, or the ways practitioners' work is made visible to those study-ing it; (2) decomposition, or ways practice is broken down into parts so that nov-ices can see, discuss, and enact the work in manageable ways; (3) approximations, or simplified teaching opportunities that are very similar to the real thing, which provide opportunity for specific feedback from instructors; and (4) documenta-tion or "conceptions of quality," which include specific criteria that define effective practice and how those criteria should be applied in a variety of contexts. Teaching is integrative work (Ball, Sleep, Boerst, & Bass, 2009); the task in a practice-based curriculum is to decompose content into teachable elements in ways that maintain its integrity and avoid fracturing it into bits that cannot be reconnected. Using the enhanced framework in the curriculum decision-making model means that all tasks, methods, activities, and content must be able to be decomposed into smaller pieces whose content and processes can be identified, studied, taught, and rehearsed, and then reintegrated in the actual work of teaching. Such efforts need to be documented over time to determine quality growth.

High Leverage Practice and Core Literacy Practices. The precepts of high leverage practice and core literacy practices are interrelated. As will be explained in Chapter 3, high leverage practice is defined by a set of research-based charac-teristics that highlight the elements of teaching most likely to achieve the instruc-tional goals and result in students demonstrating the desired learning outcomes (Ball & Forzani, 2010; Ball & Forzani, 2010/2011). Core practices occur with high frequency in teaching, are used across various disciplines and curricula, and are research-based and learnable by teacher education students, allowing interns to learn about both students and teaching (Grossman, Hammerness, & McDonald, 2009). The characteristics of high leverage practice became a lens for examining, assessing, selecting, and implementing the teaching of core literacy practices that were represented in videos and other records of practice used in the program. We identified six characteristics of high leverage practice:

1. the lesson must engage students in substantive learning;
2. the lesson must result in evidence of significant advances in learning;
3. teaching practices must have warrant in research and accepted theory;
4. activities, tasks, methods, and procedures included in the lesson must have merit in a variety of contexts;
5. the lesson must demonstrate the intern's strategic implementation of an instructional activity, practice, method, or procedure; and
6. the practices used must promote the development of higher order thinking.

When the characteristics of high leverage practice become the prism through which to analyze and evaluate core literacy practices, they shift our view of course and program content away from "coverage" to identification of essential content that leads to a deeper level of learning and understanding. Studying core literacy practices within rigorous implementation of course content enables interns to develop proficiency with the intertwined knowledge and skills involved in the actual work of teaching. The use of core practices further elaborates interns' understanding of what it means to think and act as teachers, thus developing their professional identity. By ensuring interns' proficiency with a subset of core literacy practices (described in Chapter 3), we can better define what it means to be a competent beginning teacher.

Intellectual Character and Dispositional Thinking. Our view of teaching encompasses an intellectual dimension: It is work that requires deep knowledge, constant decision-making, and complex reasoning (Lampert, 1985; Leinhardt, 1989). We wanted to explicitly attend to interns' development of this intellectual dimension; thus, the precept of intellectual character became an additional filter for selecting the core practices that were our curricular focus. Intellectual character is "an overarching term to describe a set of dispositions that not only shape but also motivate intellectual behavior" (Ritchhart, 2004, p. 31). These dispositions—curiosity, open-mindedness, metacognition, the seeking of truth and understanding, strategic thinking, and skepticism—capture the depth and breadth of good thinking. Ritchhart's is not a definitive list, but rather identifies a set of thinking dispositions that are appropriate for developing not only students' intellectual capacity, but also our interns' ability to become high quality educators. We wanted interns to engage in dispositional thinking when applying, analyzing, and evaluating core literacy practices, thus helping them establish an overarching set of behaviors. Furthermore, developing intellectual character helped interns approach core practices not in a perfunctory, inflexible manner, but rather in a way that motivates, activates, and directs their abilities. This is what engagement in the development of intellectual character means: It is more than exhibiting the desire and will to teach; rather, it is linking the enactment of dispositions to requisite teaching ability with an emphasis on quality and rigor.

Applying the precept of intellectual character to our curriculum decision-making model focuses attention on the creation of a "body of habits that developed into active dispositions (e.g., curiosity, open-mindedness, reflection)" (Dewey, 1933, p. 44), which in turn direct interns' actions, because dispositions not only shape but also motivate intellectual behavior. The effective use of a graphic organizer, for example, cannot be characterized as perfunctory and procedural; rather, effective teachers design and implement a graphic organizer in a deliberate, intentional, and strategic manner driven by dispositional patterns of behavior that are under their control and will. Without intellectual character, our actions would be an untied bundle of isolated acts, because if our habits are formed in an incoherent manner, our behavior will be incoherent. Engaging in the creation of intellectual character becomes a way of thinking in an integrated manner. Developing intellectual character and the attendant set of dispositions that not only shape but also motivate intellectual behavior leads to a consistent deployment of abilities so that patterns of behavior are established over time. In other words, when teaching is guided by the dispositions of thoughtfulness, the heart of intellectual character, the result is the development of strategic practitioners who know *when*, *why*, and *how* a core practice is taught. Developing intellectual character means having the will and motivation to engage the method or practice strategically.

Essential Content

A third consideration in our curriculum decision-making process involves ensuring a focus on essential content. The field of teacher education has long grappled with the problem of determining the content for learning to teach (Grossman & McDonald, 2008; Hiebert, Gallimore, & Stigler, 2002). Teacher educators often attempt to address too much, and in the end, we are unsure whether we have identified the most important content. This is compounded by the constraints of time, which creates a dilemma: how much content gets covered versus how well the content is learned. To manage this dilemma, we return to one essential question: What do interns need to learn to be effective beginning teachers in secondary content area classrooms? Selecting course content is a process of winnowing and sifting that begins with broad and expansive ideas, theories, methods, and practices that are embodied in core practices that are at the heart of the profession. Like many teacher education programs, we use a set of standards and benchmarks to make decisions about content. We also use a thinking taxonomy to guide the design of lessons so they move student thinking from simple to complex and draw upon video records of practice to document the evolution of interns' effective teaching.

Standards and Benchmarks. The teacher education program's standards and benchmarks (see Appendix A) developed from several sources recognized by experts in the field as capturing essential learnings of the profession—what Wiggins and McTighe (1998) and Wehlage, Newmann, and Secada (1996) consider the heart of the discipline. The standards and benchmarks establish parameters that provide guidance to mediate decision-making and enable identification of core practices.

To illustrate, Standard One deals with preparation and planning for instruction and is composed of benchmarks such as creating lessons based on significant disciplinary content, sequencing lessons and activities within units, and scaffolding and modeling of instructional activities. Standard Two addresses the design and use of a variety of assessments and includes benchmarks such as the alignment of assessment tasks with learning goals and objectives, providing timely and specific feedback, and the use of self-assessment to improve learning. The standards and benchmarks are used to craft activities and to shape them. For example, each of the video assignments requires interns to reference Standard One as they prepare lesson plans. Further, video assignments require interns to use informal assessments, as indicated in Standard Two, to document student learning.

Thinking Taxonomy. The thinking taxonomy described by Anderson and Krathwohl (2001) shapes the depth and complexity with which interns encounter the teaching-related topics and ideas defined by the standards and benchmarks. Anderson and Krathwohl transformed Bloom's taxonomy (1956) into a more constructivist view of learning. This was done by converting it from a single dimension to a two-dimensional construct by including four types of knowledge intersecting with six cognitive processes. Thus, with the addition of the knowledge types, learning was seen as more interactive and less hierarchical. In other words, when developing lesson objectives or assessment tasks, we consider movement along both continuums (that is, knowledge and cognitive). Anderson and Krathwohl did this by converting these knowledge dimensions and cognitive processes into a taxonomy table, which they labeled "a thinking taxonomy." The six cognitive process levels are: (1) remember, (2) understand, (3) apply, (4) analyze, (5) evaluate, and (6) create. The continuum represents a range of cognitive complexities—understanding is more cognitively complex than remembering, applying is more cognitively complex than understanding, and so on. The knowledge dimension is comprised of four types: (1) factual, (2) conceptual, (3) procedural, and (4) metacognitive. These categories lie along a continuum from concrete to abstract.

Our goal, in terms of defining program content, is to represent the range of knowledge dimensions and cognitive processes in any particular course. For example, interns encountered instructional uses of graphic organizers at multiple points across the program. As the interns engaged in increasingly complex efforts to use a graphic organizer, they had to demonstrate the use of a range of questions across both the cognitive dimensions and knowledge types. Likewise, each core literacy practice used must attend to the cognitive dimensions and knowledge types in a deliberate manner.

Video Records of Practice. We consider video records of practice to be essential tools for practice-based education, and thus their potential use is a key factor in our curricular decisions. The literature indicates several compelling reasons to use videos in teacher preparation. Videos allow novices to visit and revisit events and artifacts of teaching. They can visualize what theories and conceptions of "good teaching" actually look like in a real classroom. They can dig into the complex layers of teaching, uncovering the decisions, actions, and teaching maneuvers that are often difficult to see. Further, videos of teaching can provide access to a wider range of teaching contexts, enabling novices to observe a variety of districts, classrooms, and students. Finally, videos support novices' reflection on their practice—they are literally able to view, discuss, and refine their own teaching, extending the benefits of fast-paced, "live" field experience that is limited in terms of time and perspectives for such reflection.

As a factor in the curriculum decision-making model, our use of video records of practice is necessarily considered in relation to core practices and program standards. Clearly, not everything that can be captured on video is worth capturing, and indeed it can be challenging to sift through lengthy footage to determine which video clips might be most useful. We support interns' selection and study of videos of teaching that represent core practices that fit with the program standards and reflect the principles of high quality professional practice.

AN EXAMPLE OF CURRICULAR DECISION-MAKING

The curriculum decision-making model is a flexible one that can be applied when initiating a teacher education program or altering components of an existing program—for example, adding new course content or revising existing assignments. The model is intended to ensure that all curricular decisions, regardless of the point of entry into the decision-making process, are consistent with the theoretical, philosophical, research-based, and practical considerations embedded in the model. When applied as intended, the curriculum decision-making model is a methodical process that results in meaningful change, as illustrated in the following example from our own efforts to revise a key assignment related to video study.

One instance of the Instructional Video Assignment required interns to video their teaching involving a graphic organizer. The use of graphic organizers had been introduced, modeled, and practiced in the secondary literacy course, and this assignment extended their use into the interns' own teaching.

In addition to more technical directions related to producing and uploading the video, interns had these assignment guidelines:

Select a 5- to 8-minute video clip of a teaching activity in which you help students review for a major test or develop a comprehensive understanding of a major concept. The video should depict how you use a graphic organizer to explicitly scaffold your students' understanding of key ideas that will be in the lesson and/or on the test. Examples of graphic organizers can be found in the Vacca and Vacca (2002) chapters as well as other readings you've been given. Also, if you discussed graphic organizers in your methods class, you may use those examples. You might also want to search the web for examples of graphic organizers that can be adapted for your instructional purposes.

As we observed interns' video-based discussions based on these guidelines, we found that many interns' graphic organizers lacked rigor and did not fulfill the criteria for high leverage practice. In many cases, interns asked students to recall information and make connections among concepts that were either plainly stated or clearly implied in the text. The learning required by students to complete the graphic organizers and participate in the debriefing discussions after completing the organizers focused on lower order thinking. We wanted to revise the assignment to elicit more rigor. To do so, we studied a typical example of an intern's response to the Instructional Video Assignment in light of the curriculum decision-making model. We examined the audio recording of the video-based discussion along with the artifacts provided by the intern: his lesson plan and the graphic organizer he had provided to students.

Jeff, who was teaching in a 7th-grade American history classroom, had created a simple, two-column graphic organizer with headings for two political parties: the Federalist Party and Jeffersonian Republican Party. The written directions were to "Compare and explain the differences between the Federalist and the Republican parties." Jeff included two additional statements at the bottom of the page:

1. Define and explain the states' rights theory and its implications.
2. Give an example of what each party believed.

To initiate the video-based discussion, Jeff framed the presentation of the video with this focus question: "What can I do to make the graphic organizer more effective at reaching higher order thinking through format as well as discussion without significantly increasing the class time needed?" Jeff and two of his peers watched the video, which captured Jeff asking questions of students to help them complete the graphic organizer. One intern observed that a number of students were "scurrying to get the answers written down," probably so that the graphic organizer could be used for their test preparation, but the students appeared reluctant to engage in discussion about the facts within the graphic organizer. The interns noted that completing the graphic organizer required thinking at the level of "remember/recall"; Jeff attempted to elicit higher order thinking through discussion based on the completed graphic organizer as he asked students to identify the consequences of the Federalist and Republican views on the ideal economy. By asking questions verbally, he also sought to make connections to present-day political parties. But, observed one intern, "They didn't remember the facts, so in order for you to move on [to higher order thinking] it was hard, and you kept having to clarify." The interns discussed the need to modify the graphic organizer so that it would support both the identification of factual information and students' higher order thinking about that information; however, they did not make specific suggestions about how to make those modifications.

Reviewing this example of Jeff's video-based discussion of teaching involving a graphic organizer, we realized that the quality of work being produced was not consistent with important elements of the curriculum decision-making model. We determined that many interns had a limited conception of the use of graphic organizers as a core literacy practice. A key conclusion among interns in the video-based discussion was that Jeff's graphic organizer required his students simply to transfer information from the text to the two-column chart. Indeed, most interns developed graphic organizers that lacked several important characteristics: They did not move students from simple conceptual understandings to more complex understandings of key content in their subject areas, and they did not move students from lower order thinking to higher order thinking. We concluded that though we had provided interns with models of graphic organizers, we had not made explicit the connection to high leverage practice (see Chapter 3).

To ensure the assignment's consistency with the curriculum decision-making model, we developed lists of characteristics for effective use of each core literacy practice. These became part of the guidelines for the Instructional Video Assignment. These sets of criteria concisely pulled together the ideas about each core literacy practice that interns might implement in their disciplinary instruction, while also providing a tool for evaluating their design and use of the core literacy practice. Figure 2.2 is an example of one set of these characteristics: the characteristics of effective graphic organizers.

Although these new guidelines clarified some key characteristics, some of the language—that applied across all five core literacy practices—still needed further explanation (for instance, what does it mean to "move students from simple to complex understanding"?). We returned to the curriculum decision-making model, and specifically the foundational precepts and emphasis on core literacy practices. We sought to ensure that interns, through their use of core literacy practices, would address essential content that would lead to the development of intellectual character and dispositional thinking. We added the thinking taxonomy as a resource for evaluating the knowledge and cognitive dimensions developed by the core literacy practice. If the interns employed the thinking taxonomy as intended, they could use it to understand the various types of knowledge (such as conceptual, procedural, and metacognitive) and the range of cognitive dimensions (understand, apply, and evaluate) elicited by the core literacy practice.

Returning to the example of Jeff's graphic organizer, we saw the impact of making explicit the characteristics of effective core literacy practices (specifically,

Figure 2.2. Characteristics of Effective Graphic Organizers

An effective graphic organizer:

1. Organizes content in a manner that moves student thinking from simple (for example, defining a concept, recognizing an example of a concept) to complex understanding (for example, applying a concept in a new situation, evaluating a policy, principle, or theory derived from the concept).
2. Scaffolds students thinking from lower order thinking to higher order thinking.
3. Extends students' thinking about ideas/concepts/principles in the text to broader contexts (for example, connections to other texts, links to other significant disciplinary content, connections to important theories).

When implementing, remember:

1. A graphic organizer is not a worksheet to be completed; it is a well-thought-out thinking structure that improves comprehension of disciplinary content.
2. A graphic organizer weaves thinking into the fabric of the classroom, making thinking visible for learners and improving their thinking dispositions.

---

the characteristics of effective graphic organizers featured in Figure 2.2) in a subsequent instance of the Instructional Video Assignment. To our delight, in this round of video-based discussions, another intern, Meredith, had taken Jeff's original graphic organizer and adapted it in light of the revised guidelines for use with her own middle school students in an American history course (see Figure 2.3). In contrast with Jeff's two-column chart and broad direction to "compare and explain the differences," Meredith's graphic organizer provided scaffolding so that students could identify explicit attributes that defined each political party. Meredith also added questions below the chart that supported students' engagement in higher order thinking about the identified attributes.

Meredith's revision was quite a contrast to Jeff's original version. Recall that Jeff's simple, two-column graphic organizer did not call for higher order thinking, but only required students to recognize or understand the content in the text and transfer it to the graphic organizer. Meredith's revised graphic organizer and the related questions, on the other hand, addressed all four types of knowledge. Factual knowledge is addressed by the inclusion of the critical attributes (role of government and economic views). Conceptual knowledge is represented by the concepts of Federalist and Jeffersonian Republicans. Procedural and metacognitive knowledge are represented by the questions: *Did the graphic organizer help you answer the questions? If so, how? If not, what changes would you recommend?* To respond, students must judge the success of their own strategic knowledge of the procedural steps (that is, the scaffolding embedded within the graphic organizer) to determine if they helped them better understand the content they were studying (metacognitive knowledge).

Figure 2.3. Revised Graphic Organizer

	Role of Government	Economic Views	Views on Foreign Policy	Views of Slavery
Federalists				
Jeffersonian Republicans				

- Given the information above, which policies would the Federalist Party support and which policies would the Jeffersonian Republican Party support?
  1. Strong anti-British foreign policy—Why?
  2. Belief in a strong central government—Why?
  3. Strong support for a states' rights view of government
  4. Support for strong tariffs
  5. Support for the expansion of slavery
- Given the mood of the country during the election of 1800, an election where the Federalists and Jeffersonian Republicans faced one another, who might win? What evidence can you cite that supports your views?
- Given the two parties that exist today, the Republicans and the Democrats, which one would be closer to the Federalists and why?
- Did the graphic organizer help you answer the questions? If so, how? If not, what changes would you recommend?

Meredith's graphic organizer also uses most of the cognitive dimensions. Completing each of the cells in the graphic organizer requires students to both remember and understand the information presented in the text. This is illustrated by the information students must supply in the cells "Role of Government" and "Economic Views." They must analyze information to address the questions: *Given the mood of the country during the election of 1800, an election where the Federalists and Jeffersonian Republicans faced one another, who might win? What evidence can you cite that supports your views?* To answer these questions, students must break the information they supplied in the graphic organizer into its constituent parts and determine how the parts relate to one another by distinguishing relevant from irrelevant information. Another question requires an evaluative judgment: *Given the two parties that exist today, the Republicans and the Democrats, which one would be closer to the Federalists and why?*

This example illustrates how, as we modified the Instructional Video Assignment in light of the curriculum decision-making model, interns were better able to design core literacy practices to address essential content and scaffold higher order thinking—that is, they met the criteria of effective core literacy practices.

This example also illustrates the interrelatedness of the components of the curriculum decision-making model. By using the thinking taxonomy, for example, we also attended to the development of intellectual character (a foundational precept), because thinking routines (Ritchhart, 2004) lead to the evolution of thinking disposition, which is critical to the development of intellectual character.

Importantly, our efforts to revise this specific assignment also had implications for how we approached the use of video—specifically, what videos of teaching should include in order to enable the most productive discussions among interns. As we revised the assignment, we also sharpened the relationship of the Instructional Video Assignment to the characteristics of the enhanced framework. Already, the Instructional Video Assignment involved representation, as it centered on videos of the interns' teaching. However, our study of Jeff's video-based discussion indicated that the initial assignment did not lend itself to interns' work on meaningful decomposition of the use of a graphic organizer. Studying their teaching in relation to the newly explicit assignment guidelines allowed interns to peel back the complex layers of teaching so they could be examined and discussed in more detail. In terms of approximation, the teaching of the core literacy practice was highly supported and structured with the new assignment guidelines. Interns planned their graphic organizer lessons within the instructional framework provided by their mentor teachers. They designed the lesson to meet the explicit characteristics outlined in the revised assignment guidelines to support the mentor's selected content and unit. Finally, the revised assignment guidelines provided stronger support for quality analysis as interns addressed the elements of high leverage practice and engaged in repeated efforts at using this core practice. The relationship to documentation was also improved, as we were able to consider how and whether interns acquired specific competencies over time.

Hopefully, this example illustrates two important points: first, how the added value of using the curriculum decision-making model to rethink *how* and *what* it is we teach results in the enactment of a practice-based teacher education curriculum than is driven by core practices; and second, how the model is best applied in a recursive rather that a linear manner, because it is a dynamic and interactive process and not a static and inflexible one. The end result was an assignment that was stronger and more consistent with our vision of teacher preparation.

CHAPTER 3

Core Literacy Practices
and the Characteristics of
High Leverage Practice

Two important themes emerged from Chapters 1 and 2 that underscore our argument for using video study within a practice-based curriculum. The first theme was that we need a practice-based curriculum for teacher education that is driven by a curriculum decision-making model that addresses questions such as: What do novice teachers need to learn in order to become competent beginning teachers? What specific approaches and settings work best to prepare and support novices as they do the complex relational, psychological, social, and intellectual work of teaching (Ball, 2011)? We see core practices—the recognizable routines, approaches, or activities that form the foundation of effective teaching—as a central feature of such a practice-based curriculum. As Grossman, Hammerness, and McDonald (2009) cogently point out, "Focusing on core practices within teacher education provides teacher educators with the opportunity to address teaching as a complex task, while also enabling them to focus on key components with novice teachers" (p. 8).

As they study and enact core practices, novices are able to attend to both conceptual and practical aspects associated with any given practice. They can learn ways of moving, speaking, and organizing in tandem with the concepts, principles, and theories from pertinent subject areas that make the practice meaningful. In doing so, they begin to develop a professional identity around the role of teacher—that is, the practices help elaborate their understanding of what it means to teach. Professional knowledge and identity are thus woven into core practices.

The second important theme was that a practice-based curriculum for teacher education should be consistent with a theoretically and conceptually sound framework. As was mentioned in Chapter 1, we drew upon the framework proposed by Pam Grossman and colleagues (Grossman, Compton, Igra, Ronfeldt, Shahan, & Williamson, 2009) and augmented by Moss (2011), which we refer to as the enhanced framework (representation, decomposition, approximation, and documentation). Together with the concept of core practices, the enhanced framework supports a view of teacher education in which the integrated knowledge, skill, and professional identity of teaching are developed as novices learn to teach (Grossman & McDonald, 2008).

Of course, not every core practice can—or should—be learned by a novice in a teacher education program. Our challenge was to determine a manageable subset of core practices (1) that were truly essential for competent beginning secondary content area teachers to know and (2) with which the interns could gain competency within 1 year. We knew we wanted to focus on developing interns' competency with practices that address secondary students' disciplinary literacy. We needed a systematic, research-based procedure for sorting and prioritizing core practices to determine those that are critical to competent beginning secondary content area teachers' development—what we call "core literacy practices."

The basis for this sorting process was a set of research-based characteristics of high leverage practice. The characteristics are vital for designing learning experiences, assessing teaching, and reflecting on and improving teaching (Grossman & McDonald, 2008). The characteristics of high leverage practice are a means by which teacher educators can identify the essential activities of teaching and make decisions about the core practices with which novices will need proficiency to become strategic practitioners. In the next section, we discuss early work related to the notion of high leverage practice and more recent research that served to identify and validate specific characteristics. We describe our own process of developing a usable set of characteristics that we used both to inform the curriculum and to guide interns' video-based discussions of teaching.

THE RESEARCH BASIS FOR HIGH LEVERAGE PRACTICE

Early Connections

In the business world, the term *leverage practice* means any technique used to multiply gains and losses. Used in an educational context, it has a similar meaning: Educators leverage practice to improve learning. Marzano and colleagues were among the first to refer to *high leverage* as a term associated with teaching practices (Marzano, Pickering, & Pollock, 2001). They identified 10 high leverage strategies that they believed improved student achievement across all content areas and across all grade levels (including summarizing, identifying similarities and differences, and generating and testing hypotheses). In the field of English language arts, educators referred to high leverage practices as deep-rooted knowledge and skills that exemplary teachers possessed, which could serve as a model for beginning teachers (Grossman, Barker, & Brown, 2012). However, other than the general use of the term *high leverage practices*, there was no attempt to explain what it meant or how it might be used in a systematic and continuous manner (Leinhardt, 2004). As with the work of Marzano and colleagues, this early use of high leverage practice did not provide the detail or practice-based examples that would support the building of a teacher education curriculum or course.

Recent Research

Although *high leverage* appeared as a term in the literature, it was not specified as principles that could be used to identify core practices. The term *high leverage practice* gained new, elaborated meaning as the School of Education at the University of Michigan began to revise its teacher preparation program beginning in 2005. Under the leadership of Dean Deborah Lowenberg Ball, the Teacher Education Initiative was formed to create a new model of teacher education (Ball & Forzani, 2010/2011; Teacher Education Initiative Curriculum Group, 2008). As part of the Teacher Education Initiative's work, a group of University of Michigan–based researchers, teachers, and curriculum developers created a comprehensive list of more than 200 teaching techniques, strategies, and activities drawn from the content of a variety of courses. The list was narrowed to 19 practices (such as leading a whole-class discussion, eliciting and interpreting individual students' thinking, and communicating about a student with a parent or guardian) that met the group's definition of high leverage: "that is, practices that significantly increased the likelihood that teaching would be effective for students' learning" (Ball & Forzani, 2010/2011, p. 42).

Concurrent with the identification of practices that could be considered high leverage, researchers began to focus more and more on *how* to identify those practices. It became clear that, along with naming the practices, there needed to be a set of characteristics that could guide their identification in a more systematic manner, one that captured what it meant to be a high leverage practice. Those conducting the research were aware of the potential problem of grain size. It was important that the work of teaching not become overly parsed and articulated (Grossman & Shahan, 2005). Still, choices had to be made that emphasized some aspects of teaching over others.

As the term *high leverage* as an indicator of essential practices in teaching caught on, a number of presentations, articles, and studies endeavored to identify the characteristics of high leverage practice (see, for example, Ball & Forzani, 2010; Ball, Sleep, Boerst, & Bass, 2009; Boerst, Sleep, Ball, & Bass, 2011; Franke, Grossman, Hatch, Richert, & Schultz, 2006; Kazemi & Hintz, 2008; Kazemi, Lampert, & Ghousseini, 2007; Sleep, Boerst, & Ball, 2007). In one instance, Sleep, Boerst, and Ball (2007) identified several characteristics of high leverage practice in their study of the content of a math methods course guided by practice-based considerations. They identified high leverage practices as those that:

1. occurred frequently in a variety of subject-areas (for example, the writing process, the scientific method);
2. applied across different approaches to teaching subject-area content (such as understanding causality in history);
3. supported work that is central to the subject area;
4. helped improve the learning and achievement of all students (for example, methods shown to be effective, such as the use of graphic organizers);

5. could be articulated and taught;
6. were accessible to novice teachers;
7. could be narrowed and broadened for meaningful work in a semester-long course; and
8. could be practiced by beginners in their field-based settings.

These characteristics became a foundation for others to elaborate upon and modify (Ball, 2011; Ball & Forzani, 2010/2011; Grossman, Hammerness, & McDonald, 2009; Teaching Works, 2014). From these writings emerged an evolving list of guiding characteristics of high leverage practice that moved beyond an overly broad definition to a refined set of characteristics and practices. In addition, these collective lists reveal considerable overlap, resulting in a number of similarities among the work of various researchers seeking to identify the characteristics of high leverage practice for teacher education. Grossman, Hammerness, and McDonald (2009) note that all definitions of high leverage practice emphasize:

- Practices that occur with high frequency in teaching,
- Practices that novices can enact in classrooms across different curricula or instructional approaches,
- Practices that novices can actually begin to master,
- Practices that allow novices to learn more about students and about teaching,
- Practices that preserve the integrity and complexity of teaching,
- Practices that are research-based and have the potential to improve student achievement. (p. 7)

This emerging consensus provided us with the beginning point for identifying a list of our own characteristics of high leverage practice that were appropriate for effective teaching in secondary content areas and consistent with the enhanced framework.

IDENTIFYING PROGRAM-SPECIFIC
CHARACTERISTICS OF HIGH LEVERAGE PRACTICE

In making choices in our work with videos of teaching, we sought to focus on practices most likely to equip interns to accomplish fundamental elements of professional work that were unlikely to be learned through experience. From the list of characteristics of high leverage practice identified by researchers, we compiled a subset for their functionality in relation to our goals for video-based discussions of teaching in secondary content area classrooms. We selected five characteristics that aligned with the demands of secondary content area teaching and with our program and courses. We also added a sixth characteristic: higher-order thinking.

Although higher-order thinking seemed to be implied in some of the other characteristics identified by researchers, we believed that novices needed to explicitly attend to higher-order thinking in order to use it successfully in their teaching. These six characteristics of high leverage practice became part of our framework for video-based discussions of teaching.

1. ***The lesson must engage students in substantive learning.*** In order for a task or activity to qualify as producing substantive learning, it must be grounded in meaningful, thoughtful, and worthwhile content. High leverage practice provides opportunities for students to engage in learning experiences that deepen their understanding of significant disciplinary content. The learning that results from high leverage practice should build schema and help students conceptualize major ideas, principles, generalizations, and theories that are at the heart of their disciplines and should prepare students to generate new applications of that knowledge. In this way, it builds substantive understandings that students can apply to new learning situations. In applying this characteristic to their own practice, novice teachers must incorporate significant content into the lesson, and when the video is viewed, those observing it must see evidence that significant content has been taught.

2. ***The lesson must document significant advances in learning.*** This characteristic highlights the essential relationship between teaching and learning—one that may be overlooked by novices who are often deeply concerned about simply getting through a lesson plan within a given period of time. At some point during instruction, evidence must be collected or observed that documents individual student understanding of significant content. In some instances, such as an active lecture or discussion, such documentation may seem challenging. The feedback students provide during lecture is observable evidence of learning; however, it may not document all students' learning, so supplemental assessment tasks (such as exit slips) should be employed to obtain feedback from individual students. This particular characteristic of high leverage practice is difficult to capture on video, so we ask interns to include work samples that document student understanding. The interns must include within their lesson plans informal assessment tasks that are designed to gather performance data that can be used to document individual student learning. Those who view the video can then study selected samples of individual student work to verify student learning.

3. ***The teaching practices must have warrant in research and accepted theory.*** High leverage practice must not only be supported by research; it must be research that is validated by others. Rather than relying on one or two studies that document a practice, we want our interns to acknowledge a strong and compelling research base for the strategies and activities they choose to teach. In cases where research is not available to support an instructional practice,

interns should be able to link it to accepted and vetted theory, meaning that instruction based on the particular theory has been shown to produce results.[1] We require interns to justify each selected strategy, task, method, or procedure with references to appropriate research and/or theory. They explain these references in their lesson descriptions so that those who view the video can read and determine their appropriateness.

4. **The activities, tasks, methods, and procedures included in the lesson must have merit in a variety of contexts.** The learning activities, tasks, methods, and procedures that novice teachers select must be able to be enacted in a diverse range of classrooms, across a variety of curricula, and with a variety of learners. For example, the instructional practice should be effective whether one is teaching 7th-grade students or 12th-grade students. It is effective in low resource schools as well as high resource schools. It can be used to teach content in algebra as well as geometry, or American history as well as economics. It is effective when working with struggling learners as well as proficient learners, native English speakers as well as English language learners, and first-year world language students as well as those in their fourth year. An instructional practice with merit in a variety of contexts can be used repeatedly throughout the year as long as it is appropriate for the task and the content being taught and is used strategically (see Characteristic 5 below for an explanation of "strategic"). In their lesson descriptions, interns must identify tasks, strategies, methods, and procedures that are viable in other learning contexts and justify their selection to those who view the video.

5. **It demonstrates the novice's strategic implementation of an instructional activity, practice, method, or procedure.** Strategic implementation means that the activity, practice, method, or procedure is effective in reaching lesson objectives and increasing student depth of knowledge. It demonstrates a novice's ability to know *when* to use a specific instructional activity, practice, method, or procedure within a particular lesson; *how* to implement it based on the appropriate procedural knowledge; and *why* it is important to the learning goals of the lesson. This characteristic of high leverage practice moves novice teachers away from thinking about simply finding an activity to use toward reasoning about when an activity is appropriate to use, how it is done, and why it will work in the particular instructional sequence. It moves teacher decision-making away from selecting a task because others have recommended it and toward thoughtful implementation. In the lesson description, interns must articulate the when, how, and why of strategic implementation as they select a particular activity or method. Those who view the video can then determine if the activity or method is consistent with the characteristics of strategic implementation.

6. **Practices promote the development of higher order thinking.** The learning experience should require students to engage in higher order thinking[2] by

applying content knowledge to new situations, analyzing and evaluating aspects of the content being taught in order to develop deeper understandings of enduring ideas and concepts in the discipline, and generating new understandings through the creation of new knowledge. Moving to higher order thinking often requires scaffolding. Research indicates that teachers who successfully provide students with scaffolding or instructional support help them better understand how to learn difficult tasks (Perkins & Ritchhart, 2004). When planning lessons, interns must ensure that there is a balance between lower order and higher order thinking. Those who view the video must be able to see and document instances of higher order thinking (Ennis, 1987; Ritchhart & Perkins, 2008).

We used these characteristics of high leverage practice to determine the core literacy practices to include within courses and the program, to help document interns' growth over time, and to support interns' analysis, evaluation, and reflection on their teaching experiences.

SELECTING CORE LITERACY PRACTICES

The field of teacher education has long grappled with the problem of establishing the essential content for learning to teach. From a practice-based perspective, core practices are the primary curricular focus. Even so, teacher educators face a dilemma that is similar to one facing secondary content area teachers—how much content should be covered, and at what depth, within particular time constraints. Given the short period of time we have to work with interns, the use of characteristics of high leverage practice enables us to prioritize and identify the core literacy practices that are essential for skillful beginning teachers in secondary content area classrooms to understand, take responsibility for, and carry out to help students learn. This approach supports a shift in our view of course and program content: It moves it away from coverage to the identification of essential content that leads to a deeper level of learning and skilled teaching. We focused on five core literacy practices because they reflect the characteristics of high leverage practice, and are used frequently in the classrooms in which our interns teach.

Graphic Organizers

When we refer to a graphic organizer, we mean a type of visual aid that is used to represent and organize students' knowledge or ideas by helping them see relationships and retain information in a user-friendly format. Graphic organizers have a flexible form and can be used with a variety of subject areas. When employed properly, they provide students with a structure for abstract ideas by arranging them in a variety of ways: hierarchical, conceptual, sequential, or cyclical. In this manner, they afford students opportunities to transform information, ideas, and concepts in a visual way. Examples of a graphic organizer include a flow chart, a compare/contrast organizational chart like a Venn diagram, T-charts, and a main ideas/detail chart. The use of graphic organizers is a critical literacy strategy because graphic organizers help students synthesize information, build schema, and enhance comprehension (Alvermann, 1981, 1986).

Thinking Routines

Thinking routines are a subset of learning routines that go on in classrooms, along with housekeeping routines or classroom management routines. However, thinking routines are different, because they help build a commitment to capacity for thinking by directing and guiding student thought through the use of strategies such as "See, Think, Wonder," "Connect, Extend, Challenge," "Think, Puzzle, Explore," or "What Makes You Say That?" These strategies become thinking routines when they are used on a consistent and regular basis throughout the year. Through the use of such strategies, "students are enculturated into thinking, developing both their ability and their inclination to think" (Ritchhart, 2004, p. 110)—in Ritchhart's terms, this is what gives a class its life. It creates a culture of thinking by making thinking visible. Thinking routines are the foundation for thinking within subject-area disciplines, because they help scaffold how to engage in historical inquiry, apply the scientific method, or problem-solve mathematically. They provide a kind of compass to point the way toward building important dispositions of thinking: curiosity, inquiry, and playing with ideas. Through their continued use, they become part of the cultural fabric of the classroom.

Concept Attainment

Concept attainment is an instructional strategy that uses a structured inquiry process to define concepts and is a more in-depth approach to learning new words than traditional vocabulary activities. The process requires students to analyze the concept from a number of different perspectives, figure out its critical attributes, differentiate between examples and non-examples of the concept, generate a definition, and place it in relationship to other concepts. With the concept attainment strategy, students use cognitive strategies and both lower order and higher order thinking skills, such as classifying, identifying characteristics and relationships, testing hypotheses, and applying new ideas, while exploring the meaning of the target concept. The strategy is designed to help make connections between what students know and what they will be learning. The strategy can be used at any grade level and subject area and for almost any concept (such as grammatical concepts, historical concepts, mathematical concepts, and science concepts). The strategy is based on the seminal work of Jerome Bruner (1977), Herbert Klausmeier (1974), Dorothy Frayer (1971), and others.

Questioning Techniques

Questioning is the very cornerstone of education. For us, this means that questioning strategies must create a climate of inquiry and engagement that results in high quality, higher order thinking. However, not all questioning strategies do this, so interns must be thoughtful and judicious and avoid what Boerst, Sleep, Ball, and Bass (2011) refer to as those that fill in student thinking—that is, using questioning techniques to tell a student what he or she is thinking. Instead, we emphasize questioning strategies that make thinking visible: by asking questions that get students to clarify their thinking, challenge assumptions, elicit evidence as a basis for argument, integrate various viewpoints and perspectives in ways that challenge other students to investigate different ways of looking at the same issue, and get students to consider the implications and consequences of responses (Dillon, 1984; Fusco, 2012; Samson, Strykowski, Weinstein, & Walberg, 1987). However, questioning techniques that meet these criteria involve more than thought-provoking questions. They also include ways of engaging in discussion that builds coherently and progresses toward shared understanding. A wide range of students contributes orally, listens actively, and responds to and learns from others.

Text-Based Learning Strategies

Text-based learning strategies are designed to assist readers in gaining a deeper understanding of independently read texts. Some text-based strategies help students differentiate among the various genres and types of texts (for example, reading nonfiction, fiction, narrative, poetry, dialogue, or speeches) and the different types of text structures (such as cause/effect, problem/solution, and theory/evidence). Students can use them to adjust to the comprehension demands of each unique text structure or genre. Text-based learning strategies also involve helping students engage in close or deep reading of text by involving them in a thoughtful, critical analysis that focuses on significant details or patterns in order to develop a deep, precise understanding of the text's form, craft, and meanings (Paul & Elder, 2006). This is done by directing student attention to the text itself. It also enables students to reflect on the meanings of individual words and sentences, the order in which sentences unfold, and the development of ideas over the course of the text, which ultimately leads students to arrive at an understanding of the text as a whole.

CONCLUSION

We began this chapter by reiterating the need in teacher education for a practice-based curriculum. We elaborated the enhanced framework—including representation, decomposition, approximation, and documentation—that orients teacher educators toward the kinds of activities that will most likely prepare novices to do the work of teaching, both conceptually and practically. The remainder of this chapter built an argument for using the concept of high leverage practice to support teacher educators' decision-making about the content of a practice-based curriculum. The characteristics of high leverage practice provide a tool for selecting the procedures, techniques, and activities—those practices that are essential for skillful beginning teachers to understand, take responsibility for, and implement to help students learn—that will be the focus of the curriculum. In addition, when used in the context of video-based discussions of teaching, the characteristics are a tool for supporting novices' study of the practices and assessing their use of the practices.

We argue that the characteristics of high leverage practice are a necessary and essential tool for the development of a strategic practitioner—that is, a teacher who is able to integrate pedagogical and disciplinary knowledge and practice in a skillful, adept manner; who knows *when*, *how*, and *why* to implement a core literacy practice; who demonstrates the ability to judge accurately the quality of the core practice; who analyzes and contextualizes decision-making; and who uses professional language explicitly, accurately, and confidently to describe his or her practice or the practice of others. This concept of developing strategic practitioners by using the enhanced framework guided by characteristics of high leverage practice will be discussed in more detail in subsequent chapters.

NOTES

1. For example, constructivism is linked to cognitive theory; constructivist instruction such as project-based learning and other forms of inquiry has been used in a variety of settings and positive learning results have been well-documented.

2. Our program defines higher order thinking based on Anderson and Krathwohl's (2001) taxonomy, which is studied by every enrolled intern. We discuss the role of higher order thinking in more detail in other chapters.

CHAPTER 4

Using a Learning Trajectory to Document Novices' Growth in Video Study

In our effort to develop strategic practitioners, we have become acutely aware of the need to monitor and document preservice teachers' individual growth. As Moss (2011) argued in her analysis of two case studies of the application of the Grossman framework (Grossman, Compton et al., 2009) to the practice of preparing novice teachers (Boerst, Sleep, Ball, & Bass, 2011; Kucan & Palincsar, 2010), documentation of preservice teachers' progress was paramount. Attention to growth in novices' work with representation, decomposition, and approximation requires a quality control component. Moss argued for adding the concept of quality to the framework—that is, tracing novices' learning opportunities as they developed over time. In this chapter, we describe our efforts to document growth over time in the quality of interns' work with core literacy practices through video study. We describe the guidelines used to identify the content of this "learning trajectory" and its underlying principles, and we provide examples of how the trajectory functions as a tool for our assessment of interns' progress as well as their own self-monitoring. We then place the trajectory in the context of our approach to assessment of interns' progress toward becoming strategic practitioners.

THE IMPORTANCE OF DOCUMENTING GROWTH

Even instructional practices that appeared quite similar when described through the lenses of approximation, decomposition, and representation looked quite different when conceptions of quality and learning opportunities and assessments were traced over time. Representing these "learning trajectories"—which entail an understanding of the evolving dialectical relationships between learning opportunities and (at least intended) learning outcomes—seems essential to understanding and learning from the teaching practice (Moss, 2011).

Like Moss, we believed documentation of novice teacher growth was critical. Yet we recognized that in most cases, our assessment tasks (course assignments) did not communicate the kinds of learning we wanted our interns to demonstrate:

their progress in developing into strategic practitioners. In response to their design, interns tended to approach assignments that called for the implementation of activities, tasks, and varied pedagogical methods as course requirements for which they would get a (hopefully "good") grade. In short, they treated assignments as checklists to complete rather than as opportunities to demonstrate their deepening understanding of the work of teaching.

In working with video records of practice, interns had several assignments that required them to gather evidence of their teaching, which they then shared with peers. Early in our process of incorporating video study throughout the teacher education program, we often observed interns approaching the assignments in a rushed, seemingly thoughtless manner. We observed some interns hurriedly selecting video clips just moments before the study group was about to begin. In many cases, the focus question (which was intended to orient and focus the entire discussion) was too broad or even unanswerable in relation to the video clip. We concluded that the assignment, which was intended to help deepen interns' understanding of key elements of teaching, had become a rather perfunctory operation. Interns focused on getting a grade or merely completing an assignment rather than thinking like professionals. We had shared principles and examples of "strategic practice" with interns, but they still struggled to use our feedback to further their development. Though we could design activities and tasks with a clear end in mind, the broader picture of what all this meant in terms of moving toward becoming a strategic practitioner was not clear and was not adequately reflected in our assignments or feedback. If we wanted to document growth, we first needed to be clear about what that growth looked like and what form it would take. Following Moss (2011), we decided to design a "learning trajectory" that would communicate the characteristics of strategic practice and the kinds of growth that would indicate movement toward strategic practice.

We identified two epistemological considerations for such a trajectory: (1) its content and (2) the principles upon which it would be structured.

Identifying Trajectory Content

We began our identification of the trajectory's content with core literacy practices. Interns' facility with these essential, powerful teaching routines and strategies was critical to their preparation as competent professionals, and would be the centerpiece of a trajectory that captured growth. However, there were other considerations in terms of how core literacy practices were operationalized in the context of the teacher education program: We had to consider the impact of group-centered learning and the relationship to reflection (key elements of our approach to video study) and represent how these could develop in sophistication over time.

First, interns' work with video-based assignments designed to make the work of teaching visible and studyable was highly group-oriented. They regularly met with groups of their peers to discuss teaching in relation to videos and other records of practice. As the emphasis on observation and documentation increased, so did the focus on creating a community of learners. We observed a shift from predominantly individual learning to a more distributed kind of learning. This learning did not reside inside in any individual's head but instead was a collective body of knowledge created through professional discourse (Krechevsky, 2012). Ideas in video-based discussions were shared and revisited from different perspectives. This stimulated more learning, because conversations invariably provoked additional interpretations, questions, and thoughts. In McArdle's (2010) terms, the video study group represented a collection of persons who were emotionally, intellectually, and aesthetically engaged in solving problems, creating products, and making meaning—an assemblage in which each person learned autonomously and through the ways of learning of others by situating learning in the world of the professional educator. The understanding and awareness generated by sharing and dialoguing were wonderful tools for transmitting knowledge of the profession that no one person could accomplish on his or her own (Borko & Putnam, 1996; Feiman-Nemser, 2001, 2007; Putnam & Borko, 1997). Group-centered learning helped interns become more critical observers of their own teaching and deepened their understandings of teaching and learning more broadly (Suarez, 2006). In terms of the trajectory, then, we wanted to capture how group learning about core literacy practices progressed.

Second, the concept of reflection, which had long been a key emphasis in our teacher education program, needed to be addressed in the trajectory. We view reflection as a deliberative process of examining experience in light of the assumptions that an individual uses to make meaning of the experience (Dewey, 1933). In Donald Schön's (1987) terms, reflection is "a dialogue of thinking and doing through which I become more skillful" (p. 31). The results of one's reflection shape decisions about how to act next. When reflection on experience is weak, students' learning may be "haphazard, accidental, and superficial" (Stanton, 1990, p. 185). When well designed, reflection promotes significant learning, including problem-solving skills, higher order reasoning, integrative thinking, goal clarification, openness to new ideas, the ability to adopt new perspectives, and systemic thinking (Conrad & Hedin, 1990; Eyler & Giles, 1999). We found that making learning visible through group-centered video study contributed to the power of reflection. Our emphasis on reflection gave interns a meaningful way to speak in their own voices about the challenges they encountered and the successes they experienced in their practice. As they shared and discussed evidence of those challenges and successes with peers, they were able to consider alternative perspectives and develop a collective capacity for critical thinking, analytic reasoning, and integrative learning.

Our use of video records of practice had illuminated three important content components that needed to be addressed in an explicitly stated learning trajectory: a careful identification of core literacy practices, an explicit focus on group-centered learning, and increased use of reflection.

Identifying Trajectory Principles

The second defining element of a trajectory was its structure and the principles that guided its form. Capturing growth was the overarching principle. In other words, the trajectory must concretely answer the question: How good is good enough? Too often, interns implemented classroom practices at a procedural level without teacher educators' attention to how well they were applied and how well interns could unpack what they observed in their own teaching and the teaching of others. The trajectory would enable teacher educators, and the interns themselves, to document how interns changed over time as they grew from unfocused novices to strategic professionals.

We identified threshold concepts, or the foundational knowledge of a profession: concepts, ideas, principles, theories, and methods (Carroll, 2007; Dreier, 2003). Threshold concepts are essential because they are transformative, establish boundaries that function as parameters for the profession, and assist with the interconnectedness of knowledge that is indispensable for deepening critical understandings by helping novices integrate and reinterpret their previous learnings (Meyer, Land, & Baillie, 2010). They function as a portal through which novices must pass to gain entrance into a profession. The threshold concepts that informed our trajectory were captured by the foundational precepts (enhanced framework, core practices, intellectual character) and essential content (standards and benchmarks, thinking taxonomy) within our curriculum decision-making model. We wanted to ensure that interns demonstrated this foundational professional knowledge, which would indicate their readiness to teach independently and effectively.

Using our curriculum decision-making model, we designed the trajectory to monitor growth and provide interns with a sense of their progress. Early on, interns' awareness and application of this knowledge was usually incipient or rudimentary (see Figure 4.1). They did not understand in the way that a strategic practitioner would understand and apply teaching knowledge and skills, because the novices had not yet acquired the essential threshold concepts. As interns became aware of threshold concepts and progressed through the various phases, they developed a sense of where they were as they advanced toward entry into the profession. Their deepening knowledge marked their movement toward strategic "ways of thinking and practicing."

Figure 4.1. Phases of Change

Unfocused → Rudimentary → Practiced → Strategic

Notably, the trajectory sets boundaries for how one thinks and operates within a professional community. The structure of the trajectory must make clear and be explicit about how one gains entry into the profession. Thus, it has a gatekeeping function: Teacher educators can readily monitor novices' progress in learning to teach and assess their readiness to begin their careers.

Finally, the trajectory must capture the interconnectedness of threshold concepts and ideas that are foundational to entering a profession. When novices pass from one phase of the trajectory to the next, the threshold concepts are reworked, allowing them to be thought about in new ways. This has the effect of deepening knowledge, which facilitates the application of new ideas (Richmond, Juzwik, & Steele, 2012). This interconnecting knowledge of teaching creates a roadmap and accompanying indicators that assist in the identification of quality markers, driven by consideration of the enhanced framework. As we considered the design principle of coherence/cohesion, it was clear to us that the content of the trajectory (such as core literacy practices) had to be presented in an interconnected manner to enable the acquisition of deeper and richer knowledge and skills as interns moved along its continuum. For example, as interns worked with the core literacy practice of concept attainment, they moved from thinking of it as a procedure, a series of steps to be applied, to thinking of it as a procedure that must be applied at a specific point in the lesson (*when*) and for a specific reason (*why*). As their understanding developed, a new integration of thinking occurred. This helped obviate the fragmented nature of viewing activities, tasks, and pedagogical techniques as isolated bits of information (Davies & Mangan, 2007; Dreier, 2003). In this capacity, the trajectory functioned much like a schema: an organizing frame that gave shape and rationale to other ideas, theories, and principles that were foundational to the community it represented.

To recapitulate, a good trajectory must be transformative by helping interns think about the profession in new ways, must provide a "roadmap" that guides interns through their learning, must serve as a gatekeeper to the profession by making expectations clear and explicit, and must create a professional community by establishing parameters and boundaries that facilitate the deepening of professional knowledge. Most important, all of this must be done with an emphasis on quality.

USING THE LEARNING TRAJECTORY IN VIDEO STUDY

Our foremost goal was to develop a trajectory that explicated in a general manner what it meant to become strategic practitioners. As we considered the content and principles of a trajectory in conjunction with the curriculum decision-making model, we identified five attributes that were at the heart of our vision of a strategic practitioner:

1. being able to integrate pedagogical and disciplinary or subject-matter knowledge seamlessly into their practice in a skillful, adept, and efficacious way (that is, integrating content and threshold concepts);
2. knowing *when, why,* and *how* to implement activities, tasks, strategies, and methods in a strategic manner (that is, consciously applying core literacy practices in a reflective manner);
3. being able to evaluate their practice and the practice of others accurately (that is, judging the quality of an act of teaching);
4. using professional language to describe their practice (that is, collectively developing professional dialogue and building shared understanding); and
5. being able to engage in critical reflection about their own practice (that is, using self-evaluation).

These five attributes shaped the overall trajectory (see Figure 4.2), providing a framework for the specific scoring guides we developed for the various video study assignments. In what follows, we contrast the "Unfocused" and "Practiced" levels of the trajectory with examples of video discussions.

Illustrating an Unfocused Video-Based Discussion

The following excerpts from a video-based discussion illustrate an unfocused conversation. The discussion of the video tends to be scattered. Often, the group deviates from the designed topic, which results in a conversation about a generic practice rather than one on the specifics of the core literacy practice being implemented. The group also draws on pedagogical and disciplinary knowledge in an inconsistent manner. There is little or no evidence that they understand or can articulate how, when, or why the intern chose to use the particular core literacy practice. In an unfocused video discussion, there are likely some judgments about its quality; however, the use of professional language is infrequent or inaccurate.

Figure 4.2. Trajectory of Expectations
_____

Unfocused

Execution of core literacy practices lacks cohesion and is confused at times; discussions of core literacy practices are inconsistent and lack sufficient evidence to support claims, and there is little or no evidence that the intern understands the when, why, and how for selecting and using core literacy practices; the quality of the evidence used to support claims and warrants about core literacy practices is often ineffective and inaccurate; the use of professional language when describing core literacy practices is imprecise, inconsistent, and overly general; and critical reflection lacks clarity, with no explicit indication of lessons learned from observing, discussing, or enacting core literacy practices or making reflections that lead to action.

Figure 4.2. Trajectory of Expectations (continued)

Rudimentary

Execution of core literacy practices is basically at the procedural and conceptual level; discussion of core literacy practices is uneven, with some inaccuracies; there is little or minimal evidence to support claims or that the intern understands the when, why, and how for selecting a particular core literacy practice; the quality of the evidence used to support claims and warrants about core literacy practices is ineffective because of its inaccuracies, inconsistencies, and unreliability; the use of professional language when describing core literacy practices is not always precise about the implementation of core literacy practices; critical reflection reveals some lessons about the implementation of core literacy practices and includes some reflections that lead to action.

Practiced

Core literacy practices are aligned with critical subject-matter content and are delivered in an integrated, practiced, and proficient style that makes the connection between the practice and the critical subject-matter content clear to the learner; there is some general evidence that the intern can consistently, efficiently, and accurately address the *why*, *when*, and *how* for implementing core literacy practices but sometimes confuses the three; the intern also provides sufficient warrant and synthesizes, analyzes, and evaluates conclusions drawn from records of practice; the intern uses evidence appropriately, reliably, and in a consistent manner, and the criteria for selecting evidence are clear; the intern uses professional language that is precise and mostly accurate to describe the implementation of core literacy practices, and this is done with some depth; reflections offer critical insights that connect concepts, ideas, and theories in a thoughtful and insightful manner, and the intern provides several detailed examples for improving practices that lead to action.

Strategic

Core literacy practices are aligned with significant subject-matter content and are delivered in a seamless and skillful manner that makes the connection between the practice and the subject-matter content clear to the learner; there is explicit evidence that the intern can accurately and skillfully explain the *when*, *why*, and *how* for implementing core literacy practices and uses evidence consistently, efficiently, and accurately to provide sufficient warrant by skillfully and precisely synthesizing, analyzing, and evaluating conclusions drawn from records of practice by using evidence strategically in a deliberate and thoughtful manner; the intern judges the quality of evidence effectively and appropriately to support claims and warrants and this is done in a reliable, skillful, and accurate manner by employing clear and explicit criteria for selecting evidence; the intern uses professional language concisely and accurately to describe the implementation of core literacy practices, and this is done with depth and specificity; reflections demonstrate a critical, in-depth ability to connect concepts, ideas, and theories in the strategic implementation of core literacy practices, and the intern offers several insightful, detailed examples for improving teaching practices that lead to action.

In this example, three interns were directed to discuss the use of a graphic organizer to represent knowledge. Cindy starts the conversation by focusing on a generic teacher move—pacing—which serves to get the group off track from the very beginning; no one in the group seems to be aware of this. Although pacing may be important or useful to study, it is not intended as the primary focus of the interns' discussion because it is not a core literacy practice.

> *Cindy:* So the first one we're going to discuss is my video. My focus question is: How's my pacing? Am I moving too slow or too fast? I put this because I've had issues either talking too quickly or slowing down too much to overexplain things. So what have you guys got?
>
> *Mark:* Well, I was going to say at the 1:18 mark, it seemed like you were giving—the directions just kind of kept going on and on like what you were just talking about. It seemed like you were overexplaining it to them, to me—that—at least to me. It looked to me like they [the students] were bored and they were ready to get going. They understood it, let's go.
>
> *Cindy:* So do you think I was explaining the same thing over and over again, or was I just taking too much time with each individual detail?

As they isolate the issue of pacing from the complex work of enacting a core literacy practice, the group's ideas are procedural and generic (for example, "moving too slow or too fast," "overexplaining"). This exchange illustrates the kind of general, interpretive comments that characterize an unfocused discussion, resulting in a lack of depth and a lack of professional language. Mark's response to the presenter's request for feedback relies primarily on interpretations (as indicated by use of the phrases "it seemed like" and "it looked to me") that are unsubstantiated by evidence from the teaching in the video. Our expectation is that video-based discussions should provide sufficient support for important ideas through the demonstration of coherent, professional dialogue. Group members should substantiate their comments by providing specific evidence from the video— usually by noting the time marker, which allows the group to review and analyze the specific moments. In this unfocused example, Mark makes a passing reference to a time marker, but provides no specific details about what happened at those moments, and the group does not revisit those moments in the video.

The interns in this unfocused conversation continue to draw attention to various disconnected aspects of the teaching in the video, relying primarily on interpretive comments and speaking without regard for the core literacy practice. In the following instance, group member Tanya mentions a student who appeared to be disengaged during the lesson.

> *Cindy:* She was having fun playing with her chopsticks and I would have liked to see some answers from her.
>
> *Tanya:* I'm not sure how engaged she really was.
>
> *Cindy:* Exactly. That was one thing that I—I mean, she didn't—

Mark: She did come up with a couple of things.

Tanya: Did she give answers?

Cindy: Is it on the video?

Mark: If—I can go back and show you, but I don't think I need to. At the end there's a spot where she's like trying to talk over the girl, like I want in, I want it.

Attending to the behavior or perspective of an individual student may be a very productive focus during video study. In this exchange, however, the interns discuss this student's behavior as an isolated aspect of the video, without attention to how it manifested in relation to the complex activity in the classroom. Again, the issue was discussed outside the core literacy practice, which would have provided important context for understanding what was happening, why it was occurring, and how the teacher might respond in ways that would bring the student's attention back to the learning activity. Notably, the interns also pass up the opportunity to revisit the specific moment in the video, which would have enabled them to discuss it in a more evidenced-based way, instead of relying on their recollections and interpretations of what occurred.

In summary, the result of an unfocused video discussion is a seemingly disjointed set of ideas that do not build shared understanding among the participants. "Evidence" usually takes the form of interns' interpretations of what occurred rather than careful analysis of action, language, and environment. The unfocused discussion lacks professional language that would enable the ideas to be explored in other discussions and contexts.

Illustrating a Practiced Video-Based Discussion

Novices who discuss videos of teaching at the practiced level, in contrast to those at the unfocused level, demonstrate some of the following:

1. They integrate the pedagogical and disciplinary knowledge associated with core literacy practices in a skillful and strategic manner.
2. They accurately judge the quality of the practice they are viewing. Their judgment is supported by evidence from the video.
3. They use professional language in a clear and explicit manner. They use concepts and theories that can be generalized across particular instances of teaching.
4. They note whether the core literacy practice was implemented in a thoughtful and purposeful manner—that is, they examine *when*, *why*, and *how* to implement activities, tasks, strategies, and methods in a strategic manner.

In the following example of a practiced video discussion, four interns in a world languages group studied a video of a lesson designed to review the use of the ablative case in Latin. According to Jane, the presenter, "[T]he purpose of this graphic organizer that I had given them [the students] was to organize the different case uses by the signals for them that they can see in sentences. They were getting all the information organized in a visual way [so] that they could look at it and hopefully have it in their minds for the exam to distinguish between the uses." Jane had posted a mostly blank graphic organizer on the board and through a process of questioning the whole class, she gradually completed the graphic organizer while the students filled in their individual copies. Jane posed the following focus question to guide the group's viewing of the video: What could I have done to elicit more higher order thinking from my students with this graphic organizer? Already, the attention to the use of a graphic organizer (a core literacy practice) and the identification of a key concept in professional language (higher order thinking) stand in contrast with the previous unfocused example.

In their discussion, the interns mainly concentrate on how to improve the use of the graphic organizer so it better scaffolds the content that is to be learned. After some clarification about which graphic organizer was the focus of the particular video clip (because there were two different charts mentioned in the accompanying lesson plan), one of the interns, Mia, says she will state some "general ideas" to contrast with the way Jane used the graphic organizer, which led students to work mainly in lower level thinking:

> *Mia:* I wonder if they had to come up with a list—for instance, of everything they knew about the ablative case. And then they started to arrange those in a hierarchy themselves. . . . If you say to them, "What is an example of this?" then that's remember–recall. But if they're having to determine what those relationships are, that is procedural knowledge or conceptual knowledge.
>
> *Jane:* I think I get what you're saying. I could have the students on their own—could've had them generate a list of ablative case uses. And that way I know that all of the students are thinking this through, not just waiting for the two or three students who know all the answers to put them out there.

Mia's suggestion gets at the heart of Jane's focus question: how to elicit higher order thinking from students through the use of a graphic organizer. The ideas being developed indicate an understanding of the graphic organizer as a tool within a complex teaching environment—that is, the design of the graphic organizer certainly matters, but it is considered in relation to the subject matter under study, the teacher's choice of language, and the students' responses. To make changes that will promote higher order thinking, all of these factors need to be considered. Notably, Mia makes a distinction between procedural and conceptual knowledge (Anderson & Krathwohl, 2001). She uses this professional language in an informed and integrated manner, indicating that she has internalized important parts of the Anderson and Krathwohl thinking taxonomy.

Later in the discussion, Mia asks for clarification of the content under study by directing the group's attention to a particular student:

> *Mia:* I noticed, at about a minute [into the video], there's a girl answering your question about what conditions meet the ablative case and then she starts mentioning some other stuff, too. And I wasn't sure what those other things are that she's mentioning, if they were less important conditions or she was confusing things.
>
> *Jane:* This was actually a problem with my design. All of the things that she was saying were important conditions. They just weren't the same ones that I had been thinking about when I made up my graphic organizer. It was kind of a lesson for me in that they were equally important, just not what I myself used to understand the case usage. I had to draw more squares on the spot.
>
> *Mia:* I think that's great that you did that and you recognized it and it made me think—there's another moment at about 3 minutes where someone asks if it's the ablative of means/of instrument, and then you say, "Well, what question does this answer?" And there seems like there's confusion as to exactly what the subconcept is.
>
> *Jane:* Right.
>
> *Mia:* And so then I was thinking . . . what if [the graphic organizer] was a bit more like a concept map where students had to make explicit what those connections are?

Mia's question leads Jane, the presenter, to explain that she made an on-the-spot change to the graphic organizer to accommodate a student's unexpected ideas about the ablative case. Jane's explanation indicates that she drew on metacognitive knowledge to evaluate how well the graphic organizer was functioning in the instructional moment. Mia then pushes further on how to change the graphic organizer to better elicit students' ideas about and illuminate connections in the content under study. In this exchange about making changes to the graphic organizer, the study group demonstrates that they have moved beyond procedural considerations for using a graphic organizer to determine how, when, and why its use would be most effective in this particular case.

In this instance, the interns are concerned about whether the graphic organizer, in its present form, facilitates deeper learning of significant subject-area content. To engage in this type of analysis of the lesson requires the successful integration of content and pedagogical knowledge, which is so important to becoming a strategic practitioner. The interns frequently build on one another's comments, creating a sustained conversation; they develop a coherent set of ideas about how to implement the core literacy practice so that it scaffolds the learning of significant content.

But what distinguishes this "practiced" video discussion from one that might be considered "strategic"? One issue is that the group apparently simply accepts

Jane's assessment that her use of the graphic organizer led to students' engagement in lower order thinking. They do not examine, for example, aspects of the design of the graphic organizer that might have shaped students' responses; instead, they move directly to suggesting changes. A second issue relates to the use of evidence in the video discussion. When Mia raises particular points in relation to time markers in the video, the group accepts her interpretation of these (for example, when she says, "There seems like there's confusion"). These statements are not examined by revisiting the video or by others offering interpretations that would serve to confirm or enrich Mia's comments. A third issue relates to the use of professional language. Mia references Anderson and Krathwohl's (2001) thinking taxonomy, but the interns do not introduce any other theories or principles, an indicator of deep knowledge, to elaborate on the points they make. These are missed opportunities to extend their use of professional language and thus generalize their specific points and ideas across teaching contexts.

Hopefully, the description of the learning trajectory and illustrations of its use in video discussions make clear that our use of the trajectory has enabled a shift in the ways we monitor and discuss interns' progress in the teacher education program. In contrast to assessing video-based discussions on a case-by-case basis in terms of the criteria by which interns' work is deemed successful, the trajectory makes plain, through its explicit content and visible principled structure, how interns' progress with core literacy practices is a pathway toward becoming a strategic practitioner. It brings coherence to what novices might view as a disjointed set of assignments and activities and allows them to fine-tune their performance in ongoing video study groups. In short, the use of a trajectory makes it possible for both teacher educators and novice teachers to determine what novices currently know and can do and what they need to learn in order to become strategic practitioners. In the next section, we describe the implications of using a learning trajectory for the types of assessment tasks we designed.

ASSESSMENT CONSIDERATIONS

As our program evolved, we became concerned about how well video-based assignments provided an accurate indication of how interns grow and change over time. We asked ourselves, in light of the curriculum decision-making model, if our assignments, which we consider assessment tasks, worked together in synergistic ways to let interns "see" what they were supposed to learn and apply. Assessment should capture robust learning and be aligned with the intended goals of the program (Nitko, 2001; Shepard, 2000; Stiggins, 1994).

We used video records of practice to assess interns' enactment of core literacy practices in authentic ways, because authentic assessments make it possible to capture students engaged in the real-world tasks of teaching that demonstrate meaningful application of essential knowledge and skills (Montgomery, 2001; Tombari

& Borich, 1999). The challenge was that we had to make sure the assessment tasks captured interns engaged in the use of core literacy practices that were either replicas of or analogous to the kinds of situations faced by teachers in the field, because as Wiggins (1992) points out, this is one of the key ingredients of authentic assessments. In the language of our curriculum decision-making model, this is captured by the enhanced framework (representation, approximation, decomposition, and documentation). This was important because "Performance assessments call upon the examinee to demonstrate specific skills and competencies, that is, to apply the skills and knowledge they have mastered" (Stiggins, 1987, p. 34).

As we began to drill down into what all this meant, we were eminently aware that preparing secondary teachers cannot be about filling their heads with information that could not be readily transferred to classroom practice. One of the biggest challenges we faced when using records of practice was how best to guide interns toward deeper, robust understandings that successfully facilitated the application of the foundational knowledge that enhanced the quality of classroom practice. Our assessment tasks did not just document how accurately our interns could apply what they learned, but just as important, how accurately their growth could be assessed as they moved through the program. What this meant was that documentation must capture quality growth over time. It was clear that it was not enough to say we used authentic assessment tasks: We had to demonstrate that our authentic assessments documented quality growth throughout the program and that this was captured by our trajectory.

At this point we had only surfaced general concerns. We knew we had to be more explicit about other considerations. After much deliberation, we concluded that our assessment tasks were driven by a number of other but closely related variables and we knew that we had to explicate what these more specific factors were. Therefore, in keeping with the idea of employing high quality authentic assessment tasks, we had to ensure that our assessments of video records of practice provided interns with practical, usable information about their practice in real time.

A number of factors that were consistent with our curriculum decision-making model were pertinent to our approach to the inclusion of quality assessment tasks that documented deep and robust understandings of video records of practice. Our assessment tasks had to be systematic, comprehensive, and consistent; be dynamic, vigorous, and purposeful; provide meaningful and useful feedback; be designed to encapsulate the transfer of what had been learned to new situations; be comprised of important subject-area content; use self-assessment; and be transparent. These were not new characteristics; they were influenced by research conducted over several decades that had transmuted our thinking about assessment (Airasian, 2001; Darling-Hammond, 2000; Peters, Wixson, Valencia, & Pearson, 1993; Stiggins, 1994; Trice, 2000; Wiggins, 1992; Wixson & Peters, 1987). What follows is how we incorporated these characteristics into our use of documentation of growth.

CHARACTERISTICS OF QUALITY ASSESSMENTS

First, assessment must be systematic, comprehensive, and consistent with the views of learning embedded within the curriculum decision-making model (see Chapter 2). This meant that all assessment tasks must be aligned with core literacy practices that help facilitate the transfer of learned knowledge to new situations. Systematic and comprehensive assessments occur on a regular basis and reliably sample the core literacy practices that transpire with high frequency in teaching. This meant that all our assessment tasks were coordinated across courses in the program. For example, questioning techniques were introduced in the secondary literacy course and reinforced in several classes (for example, learning with digital records, methods courses, and the e-Portfolio courses). In all these courses, video records of practice were used to evaluate progress.

Second, all assessment tasks must be dynamic, vigorous, purposeful, ongoing, and interactive (Shepard, 2000; Wiggins, 1992). This means that assessment must be flexible; based on important strategies, methods, skills, and techniques; and based on significant, meaningful, and worthwhile disciplinary content. If assessment has all of these characteristics, it also meets the criterion of fairness.

A third characteristic of our approach to assessment is the importance of feedback. We wanted to make sure it was of high quality, meaningful, thoughtful, and useful. When assessment tasks possess these qualities, they provide interns with a sense of what it means to grow and improve, because feedback is one of the most powerful influences on learning and achievement (Hattie & Timperley, 2007). And because it is so powerful, it must be transparent (Frederiksen & Collins, 1989). Interns must have a clear understanding of the criteria by which their work is being judged. In fact, this is an important attribute of excellent performance assessments. Assessment tasks should be sufficiently transparent so interns can learn to evaluate their own work in the same way that their instructors do. Furthermore, particular properties and circumstances impact the effectiveness of feedback. Of particular importance is the type of feedback, the way it is given, and its timing.

Additionally, here is what we found most useful in providing feedback to our interns. Feedback must:

- provide interns with a "roadmap" that guides them from one level to the next; in order to do this, the feedback must clearly explain what differs from one level to the next;
- identify explicitly the content to be learned;
- be instructionally relevant;
- be predicated on behaviors that are directly observable;
- help interns progress along the learning trajectory; and
- be based on quality judgments.

Small-group video study provides a good example of how these characteristics were applied. We developed discussion protocols and scoring guides that directed our feedback on the progress interns made each time they discussed a video record of practice. From the very first time interns shared a video record of practice, we shared how the feedback aligned with our trajectory. Each lesson that was recorded was based on significant subject-area content and incorporated a core literacy practice. What we were modeling when they conducted small-group discussions was what we wanted them to practice when they were conducting their own classroom conversations.

Fourth, documenting the transfer of what has been learned to new situations is critical to assessing growth. Research studies have long demonstrated that learning is more likely to transfer when students have the opportunity to practice with a variety of applications while learning to use what they have learned in new situations (Bransford, 1979; Bransford, Brown, & Cocking, 1999; Perkins & Salomon, 1992; Salomon & Perkins, 1988). One important reason is the close relationship between a robust understanding of a concept and being able to *transfer* knowledge and use it in new situations. As Shepard (1997) points out, meaningful assessment tasks constantly demand that students demonstrate how previously learned knowledge can be assessed in new ways and call for new types of applications: Video records of practice are ideal for this situation. Critical here is the idea that if assessment tasks are to accurately document the transfer of knowledge to new situations, they must be deep and robust.

A fifth consideration that runs through the book is the importance of subject-matter knowledge. No assessment task should exclude significant and worthwhile subject-matter concepts, principles, or theories. In fact, these must be the focal point of any assessment task and must fully represent the competencies that the increasingly complex and changing teaching profession demands.

Sixth is the use of self-assessment. It has two purposes: One is cognitive, which increases students' responsibility for their own learning, and the other is to establish a more collaborative relationship between instructors and interns (Moskal, 2000). We have always found this to be a salient feature, especially with our use of video records, because intern participation in their own evaluation has very positive results. For example, we always have interns evaluate how well they think their discussion of shared video conversations went. We then compare their perceptions with our own. We find that this helps them develop a shared understanding of quality because the evaluations are based on the same metric. We do this because once our interns leave the program, we want them to be able to accurately evaluate their own teaching videos. Research has shown that students who participate in their own self-assessment are more interested in the criteria and their accuracy, and internalize the criteria and the quality of feedback (Dalal, Hakel, Sliter, & Kirkendall, 2012; Klenowski, 1995; Orsmond, Merry, & Reiling, 2013). Students also reported that they had to be more honest about their own work while also being fair with other students, and they had to be prepared to defend their opinions in terms of the evidence. This helps build ownership and "makes it possible to hold students to higher standards because the criteria are clear and reasonable" (Wiggins, 1992, p. 30). This point speaks directly to our concern for rigor.

Self-assessment also adds a metacognitive dimension to assessment tasks be-cause, according to Frederiksen and Collins:

> The assessment system (should) provide a basis for developing a metacognitive aware-ness of what are important characteristics of good problem solving, good writing, good experimentation, good historical analysis, and so on. Moreover, such an assess-ment can address not only the product one is trying to achieve, but also the process of achieving it, that is, the habits of mind that contribute to successful writing, painting, and problem solving. (1989, p. 30)

We have found that another salutary effect of self-assessment is that it so-cializes interns into the discourse of teaching. How does it do this? Through the type of assessments we use, interns are socialized into a community of practice and become accustomed to explaining their reasoning and offering and receiving feedback about their developing competence as part of a social group. This is part of the social dynamic that will be explained in subsequent chapters.

CONCLUSION

In this chapter, we talked about the value of using a growth trajectory to describe the quality of interns' knowledge about and enactment of core literacy practices as demonstrated in course assignments serving as assessment tasks. We described the guidelines, derived from our curriculum decision-making model, that we used to identify the content of the learning trajectory and its underlying principles, and we provided examples of how the trajectory is used to assess interns' prog-ress throughout the program. We discussed the theoretical foundation for our approach to assessment and then talked about using social interaction and self-assessment as tools for developing strategic practitioners.

In Part I we have explained the foundation and context in which our use of video records of practice evolved by explaining the framework upon which our program is based, the curriculum design model we use to make decisions about the content of our courses, and how we assess interns' progress with using core lit-eracy practices. In Part II, we describe how we structure video-based assignments designed to support interns' use of core literacy practices.

PART II

ENACTING VIDEO STUDY TO TEACH CORE LITERACY PRACTICES

Developing Meaningful Video-Based Assignments for Novices' Study of Their Teaching in Secondary Classrooms

At a weekly teacher educator planning meeting that took place early in our first year of making video study a central component of the teacher education program, the three of us (Charlie, Deanna, and Amy) discussed how things were going. We had reviewed a recording of a small group of interns discussing a video of one intern's teaching. We were dissatisfied. Although we had provided guidelines for interns' selection of a video and preparation for sharing the video, the discussion we had just reviewed was superficial, unfocused, and lacking depth. Deanna, who had facilitated the video-based discussion, wanted to understand why the interns focused on superficial aspects of teaching even when she tried to steer them toward more substantive issues. Our team thought that by reviewing the recording of the small-group discussion, we might discover ways to better structure the assignment so that video-based discussions would help the interns progress toward becoming strategic practitioners.

> *Amy:* This is different from my approach [as a teacher educator] right after viewing the video. What I do is usually have somebody summarize what they saw in the video. I start to ask people what they noticed. But that can lead to people taking us way off the intern's question about their teaching. Instead of summarizing, you reviewed the intern's question about his teaching.
>
> *Charlie:* I like the idea of saying, "Let's go back and make sure we understand the presenter's question before we start the discussion."
>
> *Amy:* But the conversation quickly moved to, "What if you did this instead?" And not on understanding what happened in the video. I think you want to unpack what's happening in the video before you go there. It needs to be grounded in, "This is what occurred; this is what I see in terms of student reaction and student learning. Therefore, I can make an informed statement about what might make a difference."

Deanna: Exactly. And Mark [an intern participating in the discussion] is saying, "Have they read this before? Have you talked about it before?"

Amy: He's trying to get more context. They're constantly saying, "Tell me more about what happened before this. Tell me about this particular student." Through the conversation, the context builds.

Deanna: I think there are two elements here. One issue relates to framing the [presenter's] question. The other issue is related to how the context for the video is presented. We need to think about how we can put these elements into a model that will shape the video discussions.

Charlie: It's procedures for unpacking, is what you want. We need a kind of a protocol.

Designing video-based assignments that effectively and efficiently addressed our instructional objectives was a complex process. Video, as has been noted, has characteristics that make it a particularly powerful medium for a practice-based approach to teacher education. Videos provide a lasting record; they can be collected and edited; and they enable time to reflect, collegiality, and fine-grained analysis (Sherin, 2004). A video of teaching has particular features: It addresses certain ideas, includes specific images, and uses particular language. Given these features, videos have the "structural potential" (DeSanctis & Poole, 1994) to support novices' discussion of some ideas and not others. These features, however, may or may not be appropriated by users; characteristics may be recognized, ignored, manipulated, or changed as the video is used in the classroom context. As with textbooks, manipulatives, and other classroom resources, video records of practice depend on the characteristics they have as well as how they are understood and used in a particular classroom context (Cohen, Raudenbush, & Ball, 2003). The instructional context in which videos are used matters a great deal when it comes to what and how novice teachers are able to study with them.

From the beginning, of course, we had ideas about what we wanted the interns to learn through studying videos of their teaching, and ideas about how they would do it. We grappled with providing the necessary structure to ensure that each video discussion addressed meaningful ideas in a robust way while also allowing the interns the flexibility to explore aspects of teaching that they found interesting or pressing. But the process was not just one of creating new tasks; we also wanted to account for existing content and assignments, established over many years in the program, into which video study could be more robustly incorporated. We needed to negotiate our new thinking about using video study of their own teaching with interns with the curriculum that we had carefully honed over the years. Importantly, we also wanted to keep the workload manageable both for the interns who would be preparing and presenting the videos and for the teacher educators who would be assessing their efforts. To guide us in this work, we turned to the program's curriculum decision-making model.

GUIDING QUESTIONS FOR VIDEO-BASED ASSIGNMENTS

As we sought to align our use of videos with the program's curriculum decision-making model (see Chapter 2), we used the theoretical foundation to identify guiding questions that would shape the objectives and assignments. These guiding questions represented an operationalization of the model through the practical application of threshold concepts, ideas, principles, and theories. The questions became a way for us to determine the extent to which we had consistent expectations across video-based assignments. In each case, we asked, does the assignment:

- Require use of significant disciplinary content appropriate for middle and high school learners?
- Align with the program's effective teaching standards?
- Document the intern's progress on a trajectory of professional growth?
- Ask the intern to draw on one or more core literacy practices that exhibit the characteristics of high leverage practice?
- Require demonstration of analytical and evaluative thinking?
- Scaffold the intern's learning so that completion of the assignment increases his or her ability to enact effective teaching practice?
- Require the use of increasingly complex knowledge and cognitive skills?
- Lead to interns' deepened understanding of practice?
- Require practiced reflection that results in improved teaching?
- Require use of professional language?

We used these 10 questions, elaborated below, to negotiate the complexities of developing assignments for video study. Our goal was to design assignments that were useful to novices' preparation for teaching in secondary content area classrooms, aligned with the current teacher education program curriculum, and manageable for interns and teacher educators.

Does the assignment require use of significant disciplinary content appropriate for middle and high school learners?

Disciplinary knowledge and content were driving components of our approach. At the center of each video-based assignment is the importance of disciplinary knowledge and the content it represents in the secondary curriculum. The field of teacher education has long debated the role of disciplinary knowledge and content in the curriculum. We are aligned with Shulman (1987), who argued that developing general pedagogical skills was insufficient for preparing content area teachers, as was education that stressed only content knowledge. Shulman put forth key elements of what he referred to as *pedagogical content knowledge*. These included (1) knowledge of representations of subject matter (disciplinary content knowledge), and (2) understanding of students' conceptions of the subject and the learning and teaching implications that were associated with the specific subject matter.

The secondary curriculum is driven by subject-specific content, and teachers make pedagogical decisions in relation to the content. As Shulman (1986) maintains, it is critical that pedagogical content knowledge be subject-specific. Our assignments were designed to accommodate the variations between subjects according to how each discipline structures that knowledge (Alexander, 1998). Interns worked with state standards and local district curriculum materials when identifying the content focus of their lessons. The appropriateness of the content was checked and monitored by both their mentors and field instructors who were subject-area specialists. Interns worked frequently in subject-area cohorts as they shared videos of their teaching so that they could discuss the nuances of using a particular core literacy practice to teach specific content.

Does the assignment align with the program's effective teaching standards?

Our program uses a set of five standards with associated benchmarks to designate the pedagogical content knowledge that is critical to becoming a strategic practitioner (see Appendix A). These standards are intended to represent Shulman's (1986) notion of pedagogical content knowledge—they capture principles of teachers' integrated knowledge with respect to pedagogy, students, subject matter, and the curriculum. They are a touchstone for interns throughout their teacher preparation as they reflect on their progress. Two of the video-based assignments we designed (described in the section starting on p. 65) require interns to explicitly address how their teaching reflects their progress toward meeting these standards.

Does the assignment document the intern's progress on a trajectory of professional growth?

In Chapter 4, we discussed the use of a trajectory of professional growth in relation to interns' video study of their teaching in secondary classrooms. The trajectory describes, through explicit content and a visible, principled structure, a pathway for growth toward becoming a strategic practitioner. It brings coherence to what novice teachers might view as a disjointed set of assignments and activities and allows them to fine-tune their performance in ongoing video study groups. The use of the trajectory enables both teacher educators and novice teachers to monitor what novices currently know and can do and what they need to learn in order to become strategic practitioners.

Additionally, the use of protocols that align with the trajectory has proven important in our understanding of interns' growth through video study. A protocol—a set of structured guidelines—can serve to organize video discussions, ensuring that novice teachers provide necessary information, address particular topics, and take certain perspectives. McDonald, Mohr, Dichter, and McDonald (2013), in *The Power of Protocols: An Educator's Guide to Better Practice*, point out that the significance of protocols is found in the careful details. They note that protocols enable the giving and receiving of honest feedback, analysis of complex problems, and grounding of interpretations of complex texts (for us, videos of teaching). As we discuss the evolution of the Instructional Video Assignment in Chapter 6, we will illustrate how the use of a protocol functioned to enable these outcomes and ultimately better assess interns' progress along the trajectory of professional growth.

Does the assignment ask the intern to draw on one or more core literacy practices that exhibit the characteristics of high leverage practice?

In Chapter 3, we discussed the characteristics of high leverage practice as a means of identifying the core literacy practices with which novices will need proficiency to become strategic practitioners. The study of these practices, we believe, will equip novices to accomplish fundamental elements of the professional work of teaching. Any video-based assignment must address all the characteristics of high leverage practice and require the use of one or more core literacy practices. This focus on proficiency with core literacy practices will be evident in the descriptions of key video-based assignments that follow in Chapters 6, 7, and 8.

Does the assignment require demonstration of analytical and evaluative thinking?

Through video study, interns assess the cognitive dimensions (described by Anderson and Krathwohl, 2001) that their lessons require of students. They cannot merely assert that a lesson addresses analysis and evaluation; they must be able to recognize instances of this in the teaching videos that are discussed and used as part of the various assignments. Video assignments are also structured to support interns' analysis and evaluation of core literacy practices. As Anderson and Krathwohl (2001) note, the cognitive processes of analysis and evaluation tend to receive less emphasis in educational settings, yet they are essential to novices' proficiency with core practices: Interns must be able to break the core literacy practice into its constituent parts and determine how the parts are related within an overall structure (analysis), and they must be able to make judgments about the quality and effectiveness of the core practice as implemented (evaluation). Each video-based assignment requires interns to analyze and evaluate records of their teaching in middle and high school classrooms. As will be seen in the chapters that follow, each video-based assignment was structured to enable not only illustration and explanation of interns' teaching in middle and high school classrooms, but also analysis and evaluation of the core literacy practices relative to the program standards and benchmarks.

Does the assignment scaffold the intern's learning so that completion of the assignment increases his or her ability to enact effective teaching practice?

The use of modeling and exemplars is critical to scaffolding novices' learning from video study. This allows them to envision what high quality video study looks like and to understand the specific elements of each video-based task. Throughout the 1-year teacher education program, we share and explicate examples of high quality videos of teaching, discussions of teaching videos among interns, and written reflective analyses of videos and other records of practice. For example, during the first weeks of the program, interns are asked to video a teaching episode in which they demonstrate how to use questions that guide a Title I student's understanding of a complex piece of text. Before completing this assignment, interns spend time discussing examples of effective questioning techniques, focusing on how the questions scaffold comprehension and move students' thinking from lower to higher order thinking. They study videos submitted by interns from the previous year, which allows them to critique the questioning techniques using guidelines for effective questioning and talk about how the questions achieve the objectives of the assignment. The modeling of effective questioning and analysis of previous interns' videos enables current interns to better plan their questioning techniques and successfully enact their first teaching episode.

In addition, alignment within and among video-based assignments is critical to scaffolding learning. Alignment occurs within assignments by making sure that interns recognize the characteristics and value of a well-planned lesson. Interns are required to submit a detailed lesson plan with each video. Before viewing a video, interns discuss alignment among several elements of the lesson: the purpose and goals of the lesson, the content to be taught, the objectives to be achieved, and the instructional activities used to support learning. Alignment is important because it focuses attention on how a lesson must be coherent and flow.

We also scaffold interns' learning from video study by ensuring alignment across video-based assignments. This alignment is evident in both the objectives and the expectation for how records of practice will be selected. This allows interns to see connections among the various assignments and experience video study in a structured, and therefore manageable, manner. For example, our video-based assignments share the objectives of gathering evidence and documenting progress. As they seek to gather evidence and document progress, interns can actually use the same carefully selected video for discussing their teaching with peers, illustrating their competence with a particular program benchmark, and reflecting on their progress toward becoming a strategic practitioner. Novices' repeated engagement with the same video can allow their description, analysis, and evaluation of their teaching to become increasingly sophisticated and refined.

Does the assignment require use of increasingly more complex knowledge and cognitive skills?

The Anderson and Krathwohl taxonomy (2001) provides a range of knowledge types that moves learning from simple to complex: from factual to conceptual to procedural to metacognitive levels of understanding. Their taxonomy also provides a range of simple to complex cognitive skills: from recall to understanding, to application, to analysis, to evaluation. For each video-based assignment involving a core literacy practice, we expect that interns will use the selected practice to move students' understanding from simple to complex along both of these dimensions. In one example, an intern taught and videoed a lesson that addressed how to interpret, analyze, and evaluate the content of an editorial cartoon. We shared this video with the content literacy class to illustrate how the intern's lesson moved students from interpreting the content of the cartoon (a knowledge consideration: factual and conceptual), to analyzing the perspective of the cartoon, to critiquing how the cartoon represented only one perspective of a complex issue (a cognitive dimension consideration: analyzing and evaluating). This video served to illustrate how a lesson moved thinking from simple to complex and made the point that when interns used various literacy strategies, their lessons needed to scaffold these complex moves. As interns develop and implement their lessons, we look to make sure that assignments are moving from simple to complex on both the knowledge type and the cognitive skill dimensions.

Does the assignment lead to interns' deepened understanding of practice?

As the previous example illustrates, this type of analytical approach to the examination of practice leads interns to a deeper understanding of effective teaching practice by heightening their understanding of the increasingly complex knowledge and cognitive skills that define high leverage practice. We expect that interns' construction of the assignments and their subsequent discussions of the videos of their own and their colleagues' lessons lead to a deeper understanding of high leverage practice. We expect interns to demonstrate this in a number of different ways: by analyzing and evaluating the quality of the implementation of core literacy practices through the use of effective criteria to evaluate their overall quality; by organizing the content of the assignment in a manner that moves student thinking from simple to complex understanding; by demonstrating how the assignment scaffolds student understanding from lower order thinking to higher order thinking; or by demonstrating how a literacy activity weaves thinking into the fabric of the classroom, making thinking visible for learners and improving their thinking dispositions. In each of these instances, the assignment, because of its structure and the expectations we impose, guides understanding of how to construct a lesson and then through discussion interpret, analyze, and evaluate its overall effectiveness.

Does the assignment require practiced reflection that results in improved teaching?

As in many teacher education programs, we support reflection as an essential process for novices' learning to teach. The results of one's reflection shape decisions about how next to act. Well-designed opportunities for reflection promote significant learning, including problem-solving skills, higher order reasoning, integrative thinking, goal clarification, openness to new ideas, ability to adopt new perspectives, and systemic thinking (Conrad & Hedin, 1990; Eyler, Giles, & Schmiede, 1996). Notably, the process of reflection is not an end in itself, but rather a means of developing the integrated knowledge, skills, and judgment that are essential to teaching.

We seek to nurture interns' reflective capacity so that they see reflection as an essential, ongoing aspect of their teaching in secondary classrooms. Recall that as a practice, teaching involves near-constant decision-making as teachers seek to manage the variation, interaction, and complexity inherent to instruction (Lampert, 1985, 2001). Teachers engage in reflective thought not as a protracted, prolonged effort; rather, it often occurs instantaneously in order to inform a next immediate decision. We endeavor to slow this process down for interns, particularly through the use of videos and other records of practice that allow them time to consider and reconsider teaching actions and related knowledge, judgments, and beliefs. As will be seen in our descriptions of video-based assignments in the following chapters, we use the concept of reflection within our practice-focused framework to support novices' study of and engagement in core literacy practices.

Does the assignment require use of professional language?

An important part of each assignment is how video records of practice are discussed or written about: The precise use of professional language is essential. Vague or generic language limits the possibility of extending concepts and ideas across teaching contexts and potentially creates misunderstanding. The naming of threshold concepts, ideas, principles, and theories facilitates connections across contexts and demonstrates that one is part of a professional community. Further, the use of professional language enables us as teacher educators to assess interns' understanding of concepts in relation to their teaching in secondary classrooms.

Early in our use of video study, we recognized that many interns considered "use of professional language" to mean simply mentioning the names of concepts or theorists. We wanted to move to a point where interns could associate particular learning principles with core literacy practices and then provide a warrant to support their claim. In other words, we wanted them to connect learning principles with core literacy practices so they were clear about why the practices were selected, when their use was appropriate, and how they would be taught. Interns' use of professional language, we believed, would indicate a more strategic understanding of when, why, and how core literacy practices are used.

In short, we want interns to use language in ways that both nurture and demonstrate their knowledge of the profession. This is why the use of professional language is an explicit element of our trajectory and protocols. For example, the trajectory states that to be a strategic practitioner, an intern must use professional language (1) concisely and accurately to describe the implementation of a core literacy practice, and (2) with depth and specificity that foster the development of dialogue that builds a professional community by connecting theory and practice. In every video-based assignment, we expect interns to demonstrate their knowledge of the profession by using language that clearly and accurately reflects their understanding of the work of teaching in secondary content area classrooms.

TWO VIDEO-BASED ASSIGNMENTS

We designed two pivotal video-based assignments to engage the interns in reflection, analysis, and discussion of their teaching practice. These assignments are ongoing; interns work on them periodically over the course of the teacher education program. Although the objectives and format differ, each assignment is designed to support interns as they (1) carefully select videos (and other records) of their teaching, (2) organize those selections so that they can be studied by a small group, and (3) share and discuss them with a small group. The two assignments—the Instructional Video Assignment and the Reflective Writing Task—are briefly described here. In the chapters that follow, we will elaborate on and illustrate how these assignments function in our efforts to develop effective middle and high school content area teachers.

The Instructional Video Assignment

The Instructional Video Assignment, which occurs seven times during the 1-year teacher education program, focuses on interns' teaching of core literacy practices. For each Instructional Video event, interns are tasked with preparing a video of their teaching of a particular core literacy practice to address the content under study in their middle or high school classrooms. The assignment has four parts. First, each intern selects and posts the video, along with the lesson plan, to a course website that allows classmates and teacher educators to access it. Second, the interns meet in small content-specific groups (usually three to four interns) to view and discuss the videos of teaching. As they view each participant's video, the interns follow a protocol of guiding questions, and later post an audio recording of their discussion to the same sharing site. Third, a teacher educator reviews the audio recordings and selects one or two teaching videos and related discussions that would be beneficial to the larger group as they continue to work with the core literacy practice under study. These artifacts are then shared with the entire content-specific group (usually 10–12 interns seeking certification in English, math, science, social studies, or world languages). This discussion is led by a teacher educator, who focuses on the nuances of the core literacy practice in relation to the particular subject matter as well as the richness of the video discussion among the interns. Finally, the interns write a reflective essay that describes what they learned from viewing and discussing the various video records of the core literacy practice. The essay is structured to capture interns' reflections on how they will apply what they learned to their own practice.

Reflective Writing Task

The Reflective Writing Task's purpose is to elicit analysis and application of the program's standards and benchmarks in relation to the interns' own teaching. Over the course of their time in the program, the interns are assigned to document their work on each standard and the associated benchmarks (see Appendix A) with selected videos of their teaching and other records of practice (lesson plans, student work samples, and so on). The Reflective Writing Task takes the form of a lengthy essay in which interns describe, analyze, and reflect on their progress toward meeting the standard under consideration, with records of practice embedded to support their ideas. Interns are provided with a focus question (such as, What have you learned about creating a classroom environment, and how can what you have learned be applied to your own teaching?), which is intended to enable broad, reflective consideration of the standard under study rather than a mere listing of how they could illustrate the benchmarks. Interns complete five Reflective Writing Tasks over the course of the year, one for each of the program's standards.

Notably, standards need not be the focus of an assignment like this. The Reflective Writing Task provides an opportunity for novices to use videos and other artifacts to think deeply about their own practice, learn how to unpack the complex moves of teaching, document their own progress, and engage in reflective thinking that provides a deeper understanding of the knowledge, skills, and dispositions of teaching. Any program or class outcome or competency can be easily substituted—the point is to anchor the assignment in theoretical, conceptual, and philosophical constructs that are at the heart of a practice-based approach to teacher education.

These assignments, the Instructional Video Assignment and Reflective Writing Task, are the focus of the chapters that follow. In Chapter 6, we describe the structure of the Instructional Video Assignment and go into depth about the first part: the lesson planning and the selection of appropriate videos. In Chapter 7, we continue describing the Instructional Video Assignment by talking about the discussions that take place and the protocol used to guide them. We discuss a scoring guide that was developed to monitor the growth of interns' movement toward becoming strategic practitioners. In Chapter 8, we talk about the role of reflection in transforming teaching practice and illustrate how we develop our interns' skill in critical reflection.

CHAPTER 6

The Instructional Video Assignment

Part 1—Preparation

> Analyzing video records of practice was a powerful exercise because it brought significant depth to the act of reflection. We were coached to become reflective practitioners, and reflecting at the end of a lesson or the end of a day from memory, or even with the assistance of handwritten scribbles on a lesson plan, was challenging. A well-positioned camera, however, recorded unbiased, factual data. With a reliable data set, I was able to reflect on my actual practice and make deliberate changes for future lessons.
>
> —Teacher Education Program Graduate

The Instructional Video Assignment is the centerpiece of our work with video study in secondary content area teacher education. Early in the process of developing a video-based component of the curriculum, we envisioned a recurring assignment, driven by the interns' concerns about and interest in their own teaching, that would support meaningful conversations about novice practice among small groups of peers. We sought professional, practice-based conversation that was not staged, contrived, or superficial. Over the years, using the curriculum decision-making model, we have tweaked and refined the Instructional Video Assignment and developed several tools to support interns' productive completion of the assignment. As the above quote from a graduate illustrates, it is an opportunity that most interns value.

The Instructional Video Assignment has four parts (see Appendix B for the full assignment):

1. Each intern selects and posts a video of his or her teaching with the associated lesson plan to a course website;
2. the interns meet in content-specific small groups to view and discuss the videos (the discussions are audio recorded and also posted to the course website);
3. the teacher educators select teaching videos and recorded discussions to share and discuss with the entire content area group; and

4. each intern writes a reflective essay focused on application to his or her own practice.

The interns complete the Instructional Video Assignment seven times during the 1-year teacher education program, and they also draw on artifacts and experiences from the assignment to complete Reflective Writing Tasks (see Chapter 8). In short, the Instructional Video Assignment is a pivotal video-based assignment. Although the entire assignment is relatively compact in terms of the amount of time needed to complete it, there are many elements, which is why we discuss the Instructional Video Assignment in two chapters. This chapter addresses preparation for the assignment, including interns' use of a lesson plan and selection of a video to share with a small group of peers. The actual video discussions will be addressed in Chapter 7.

THE LESSON PLAN

We have found that the preparation of a lesson plan is essential to a high quality video-based discussion. For the Instructional Video Assignment, the lesson plan is not a traditional plan in the sense of simply laying out instructional goals and steps; rather, it is a more elaborate document intended to make the interns' thinking about their teaching visible to themselves, their colleagues, and the teacher educators. Its function is twofold: to guide the presenting intern's development of the lesson and to foster conversation in the subsequent video-based discussion. The use of the lesson plan template (see Figure 6.1) is a recursive process: Interns complete it before they teach lessons that use assigned core literacy practices, and they revise it again after teaching to prepare for video discussions that can address selected, well-defined aspects of their teaching experiences. A lesson plan is posted to a course website in advance of any video discussion so it can be referenced by participants before and during the actual conversation.

This lesson plan template represents our efforts to embody the 10 guidelines presented in Chapter 5 in a document that shapes the form and content of Instructional Video Assignment discussions. In the section that follows, we address several components and characteristics of the lesson plan. First, we discuss the focus question and accompanying rationale that each intern selects to orient the video discussion (items 8 and 9 in the template). Then we address the characteristics of high leverage practice and how they are explicitly addressed in writing in order to shape the video discussion (item 10). Finally, we address several instructional elements: significant content (item 4), objectives (item 5), artifacts (item 7), and phases of instruction (item 11). We illustrate several of the components with excerpts from a completed lesson plan by Lila, an intern who taught 7th-grade English language arts. Lila's lesson plan is included in full in Appendix C.

Figure 6.1. Lesson Plan Template for the Instructional Video Assignment

As you use this template, remember that this is a recursive process in which you begin with your initial plan for instruction and then revise portions (for example, focus question, comments about high leverage practice, phases of instruction) based upon the content of the video clip you selected for discussion.

1. What is the purpose of the lesson?

2. What was taught in the previous lesson?

3. In what grade level/course was this lesson taught?

4. What concept/idea and other types of knowledge (principles, theories, models, procedures, strategies) were taught in the lesson?

5. What was/were the objective/s? In parentheses after the objective/s identify the specific knowledge level (type and subtype) and cognitive dimension (category and cognitive process) (Anderson & Krathwohl, 2001).

6. Explain how you document individual student learning.

   a. Given the purpose of the lesson and the objectives, explain how the formal and informal assessment tasks document what is to be learned in the lesson.

7. Include any teaching artifacts that are used during the video clip (such as a graphic, a handout, copies of PowerPoint slides, questions discussed, samples of student work).

   a. Include a copy of the literacy activity students complete.

      i. Specifically, how does the literacy activity used in the lesson reflect the characteristics of an effective literacy activity that accompany each assignment (for example, learning from text)? Explain the connection to each of the characteristics.

      ii. How does the identified activity facilitate the learning of meaningful content?

   b. How do the other attached artifacts help viewers better understand the focus question, and how do they help scaffold instruction?

8. Identify a focus question that will serve as a guide for the viewing and discussion of this lesson. The focus question must be directed at the teacher moves with which you are seeking help.

   a. Does the focus question have both elements (that is, the identification of the content to be learned in the activity and the specific literacy activity used in the lesson)?

   b. Given the purpose of the lesson, is the focus question appropriate?

9. Rationale: Why is the focus question appropriate for the video segment that will be viewed?

   a. Describe the context of instruction depicted in your instructional video.

   b. Which objectives are the focus of the video clip?

10. In what ways does the teaching practice depicted in this lesson represent high leverage practice?

    a. Merit in a variety of contexts.

Figure 6.1. Lesson Plan Template for the Instructional Video Assignment (continued)

    b. Warrant based on research and accepted theory:

        i. What are the underlying learning principles on which the literacy activity is based?

    c. Substantive learning.

    d. Higher order thinking.

    e. Documentation of significant advances in learning.

    f. Strategic implementation: Discuss *why*, *when*, and *how*.

11. Using the phases of instruction listed below, describe the sequence of instruction for teaching the essential content in the lesson. Also identify which phase the video clip is from.

    a. Beginning of the lesson (how the topic is introduced, how a purpose for learning is set, how prior knowledge is activated, how new vocabulary is introduced, and so forth)

    b. Middle of the lesson (how students actively engage in processing the content of the lesson)

    c. Conclusion of the lesson (how the lesson is wrapped up and knowledge learned is summarized and/or synthesized)

Focus Question and Rationale

The focus question plays a pivotal role in setting up the discussion of the video. It functions much like the essential question used by Wiggins and McTighe (2005) in their book, *Understanding by Design*. Essential questions "serve as doorways through which learners explore the key concepts, themes, theories, issues and problems that reside within the content, perhaps as yet unseen" (p. 106). For our purposes, the focus question identifies what the intern wants the group to discuss relevant to his or her use of a core literacy practice as represented in the selected video and leads to further questions that may not yet be evident to interns. We emphasize that the focus question must address two key elements: significant subject-area content and a core literacy practice (graphic organizers, questioning techniques, text-based learning, thinking routines, or concept attainment). Together, these encapsulate pedagogical content knowledge (Shulman, 1987).

    When developing a focus question, interns must think carefully about the input they want from their colleagues. The question sets up the conversation, so it is important for it to address a well-defined area of their teaching. Figure 6.2 lists three examples of focus questions.

    In the first two examples, the focus questions clearly state a core literacy practice (questioning—in this case, based on Beck and McKeown's Questioning the Author strategy) as well as significant subject-area content (structural analysis and key concepts, Atlantic Revolutions). We consider these good focus questions;

Figure 6.2. Sample Focus Questions

Subject Area	Focus Question
World Languages	Did my use of the Questioning the Author strategy for structural analysis (investigating compound words, recognizing word stems, and familiar word units) engage students in the learning of such concepts as fashion?
Social Studies	Does my lesson effectively use the Questioning the Author strategy to help my students learn what they need to know about the Atlantic Revolutions?
English	What ideas do you have for improving my questioning techniques, which I feel are really awkward?

their clarity and directness have potential to guide a solid discussion of the intern's teaching. The third example in Figure 6.2, on the other hand, is a poor focus question. It addresses generic "questioning techniques" and makes no reference to content at all. In our experience, this kind of broad and unspecific focus question leads to surface-level discussions that fail to address the complex interactions of teacher, students, and content that are at the heart of teaching.

Note that the third example is fairly typical of what interns generate at the beginning of the teacher education program. Interns initially tend to focus on general factors such as the volume of their voices, the ways they move around the classroom, or nonspecific concerns about "student engagement." As we work across the year to develop the interns' understanding of selecting significant content and introduce the various core literacy practices, we also model the development of well-designed focus questions. We emphasize, and ask interns to check, that significant content and the core literacy practice are explicitly addressed in an appropriate focus question.

To make sure the focus question aligns with the rest of the lesson, the lesson plan template also includes a rationale statement. The interns use this statement to justify how their focus question aligns with other important components of the lesson (such as objectives, significant content, purpose). The rationale serves two purposes: It further clarifies the focus question for participants in the discussion group, and it helps ensure alignment among the elements of the lesson plan. In the rationale, interns address three specific areas: (1) why the focus question is appropriate for the selected video, (2) the context for instruction, and (3) the lesson objectives that are the focus of the lesson. Developing the rationale helps the presenting intern think more deeply about the selection of an aspect of instructional practice to study with peers and the appropriateness of the video for studying this aspect of practice, as well as the influence of contextual factors on the achievement of objectives. Furthermore, those reading the lesson plan and viewing the video understand those factors as well.

In the example of Lila's lesson plan (Appendix C), the focus question is stated as follows: How well does the problem-solution structured study guide work to reinforce student application of mystery concepts and vocabulary to a new mystery (A Disastrous Dinner comic strip)? Here, Lila has identified text-based learning strategy as her core literacy practice (the problem-solution study guide) as well as the content she wants the 7th-grade students to learn through their engagement with the study guide. Lila goes on to explain in the rationale (item 9 in the lesson plan template) that she decided to use a study guide because (1) it would facilitate students' application of familiar concepts in an unfamiliar text and (2) the study guide could be designed to reflect the problem-solution structure of the mystery genre, the content under study. In short, she links the core literacy practice to lesson purpose and content. We characterize these as a well-designed focus question and a thoughtful rationale that together have strong potential to shape a productive video discussion.

Characteristics of High Leverage Practice

As discussed in the first section of this book, we employ six characteristics of high leverage practice to deepen interns' understanding of the teaching process because they provide a framework for aiding interns in unpacking their thinking about the complex process of teaching a lesson (see Chapter 3). To demonstrate the six characteristics of high leverage practice, a lesson must: (1) engage students in higher-order learning; (2) document significant advances in learning; (3) include teaching practices that have warrant in research and accepted theory; (4) include activities, tasks, methods, and procedures that have merit in a variety of contexts; (5) demonstrate strategic implementation; and (6) promote the development of higher order thinking. Interns address the characteristics in the lesson plan and then discuss with their small group how the characteristics are integrated into the implementation of the lesson. Our six characteristics of high leverage practice function as a filter that secondary teachers use to make decisions about core literacy practices, because there are too many strategies and methods from which to choose and, more important, to implement strategically. In practice, they are used in a winnowing and sifting process that expedites curricular decision-making and helps interns critique the effectiveness of implementation of a literacy practice employed in a lesson. In this section, we describe how the six characteristics of high leverage practice are used in the lesson plan template (item 10) and thus shape the Instructional Video Assignment discussions. We illustrate several of the characteristics with examples from intern Lila's lesson plan.

Substantive Learning. The lesson must engage students in substantive learning. This ensures that essential and critical content is the lesson's focal point. Interns might draw upon disciplinary references, the Common Core State Standards, or other standards documents and school district curriculum materials to determine the selection of meaningful and appropriate content. This characteristic overlaps with the information provided about the significant content addressed by the lesson (items 4 and 5 of the lesson plan template, described below).

Significant Advances in Learning. The lesson must document significant advances in learning. The lesson plan template requires the interns to provide evidence that they documented individual learning and that it aligned with the objectives and purpose of the lesson. The lesson needs to incorporate assessment of each individual student rather than relying solely on assessment of the whole group or small groups. Furthermore, the documentation of growth needs to be based on a task or assignment, rather than on general observations or impressions, which can be inaccurate, especially among beginning teachers. Many of our interns make use of student work samples that serve as informal assessment or formative assessment practices such as an "exit ticket" that is individually completed at the end of the lesson. These documents become artifacts that can be referenced during video discussions.

Documentation of student learning is particularly difficult to capture on video, but it provides important context for understanding what occurs in an instructional video. Thus, we require interns to describe their use of assessment during the initial stages of video discussion when the context for the lesson is presented. The intern must be able to explain the connection among the stated purpose of the lesson, the objectives of the lesson, the significant content of the lesson, and how these are all aligned with the assessment task. In item 6 of the lesson plan template, the interns address two prompts: Explain how individual student learning is documented, and then, given the purpose of the lesson and the objectives, explain how the formal and informal assessment tasks document what is to be learned in the lesson.

For Lila, documentation of student learning meant administration of a pretest and a posttest that addressed features of mystery texts and mystery-related vocabulary. Consider Lila's explanation of how she documented student learning after the lesson:

> The final day I administered a posttest. Students were asked to define the same five words in short-answer responses, and the multiple-choice questions were the same as well, but I moved around the answers to ensure that students weren't simply memorizing letters from the first test. The overall results were promising. Out of 60 students, only a few of them received a grade less than 8 out of 10 on the posttest, and those who did receive a grade less than this had been absent for 1 or more days of the lesson.

Lila's explanation of the content of the posttest (with the vocabulary words and multiple-choice questions being "the same" as on the assessment given before the lesson) is consistent with her emphasis on those concepts throughout the lesson. Elsewhere in the plan, Lila notes that additional assessment information was gathered through "answers and explanations in class, as well as through completion of in-class worksheets and study guides," but she does not address what she learned about students' understanding from this information. Lila's explanations of assessment were thorough in terms of the various ways that students were assessed, and in the end did demonstrate growth in students' learning. However, Lila does not explicitly address the relationship to lesson objectives. This is typical among interns and even beginning teachers: They can develop lesson plans that demonstrate alignment among objectives and assessment tools, but they may not readily examine the outcomes of this alignment in terms of student learning after they teach the lesson. This underscores the importance of using a lesson plan to shape video discussions: It makes plain the relationship between objectives and assessment so that novices can progress toward examining outcomes in a more meaningful way.

Warrant in Research. The literacy strategy used in the lesson must have warrant in research and accepted theory—that is, the intern must be able to articulate clearly the learning principles that are derived from the research associated with the selected core literacy practice. This is not a perfunctory listing of research studies; it is the justification for why the intern selected a particular literacy strategy for this particular lesson, and becomes part of the rationale described at the beginning of the video discussion. Lila draws upon Vacca and Vacca (2008), the primary text used in the content literacy course that supported interns' study of text structure guides as a core literacy practice, and also notes that her use of the literacy strategy draws upon the structure of the genre under study.

Merit in a Variety of Contexts. The activities, tasks, methods, and procedures included in the lesson must have merit in a variety of contexts. That is, the selection of a literacy strategy must be one that can be used in other subject areas and grade levels, and can be used repeatedly as long as it is appropriate for the task and content being taught and is used strategically. This is explicitly addressed in the lesson plan, and then again during the video discussion, to engage the participants in thinking about application to their own practice. Lila's lesson plan, for example, explains that the type of text structure study guide she prepared, and the process of gathering evidence and formulating a conclusion, "could be used in a history, math, or science class where the teacher provides the student with a subject-specific text and a text structure study guide (for example, cause and effect, comparison/ contrast, problem/solution) to help them organize the information they are reading." If novices recognize that literacy strategies have merit in other subject areas and developmental levels, they and their students have an increased chance of becoming more adept and skillful at using them.

Strategic Implementation. The lesson plan describes how the intern will strategically implement the core literacy practice. This lies at the heart of all the characteristics of high leverage practice because it requires interns to clearly state in their planning and demonstrate in their teaching that they know *when* in the lesson it is most appropriate to use the literacy strategy, *why* it is important to the goal of the lesson, and *how* they will go about implementing the procedures associated with the literacy strategy. They must also be able to discuss with their colleagues when, why, and how the literacy strategy makes sense from both content and pedagogical perspectives. This makes the difference between simple compliance in completing an assignment and thoughtful, purposeful planning and implementation of a lesson. In Lila's case, her analysis of why the cognitive skills embedded in the core literacy practice would aid her students' learning of important disciplinary content, her attention to the timing of when the practice would make the most difference in achieving the objectives, and the way she adapted the study guide to best address the context for instruction all demonstrate her progress toward becoming a strategic practitioner.

Higher Order Thinking. The lesson plan promotes the development of higher order thinking. The core literacy practice should be used in a way that moves student understanding from lower order thinking to higher order thinking, and this must be explicitly addressed in the lesson plan, video, and discussion. The movement from lower order thinking to higher order thinking, a transformation of cognitive complexity, takes many forms: having students apply content knowledge to new situations, analyzing and evaluating aspects of the content being taught in order to develop deeper understandings of enduring ideas and concepts in the discipline, and generating new understandings through the creation of new knowledge.

Lila's plan explains that she structured the study guide to support engagement in higher order thinking as students identify clues and characters in the text and then classify these using mystery-related concepts and vocabulary: "This moves students from the lower level of recognizing a clue (factual knowledge) to being able to classify that clue using disciplinary/subject-specific terminology (conceptual knowledge, knowledge of classifications and categories)." Notably, interns cannot merely assert or claim that the literacy strategy will produce higher order thinking; they must provide the discussion group with evidence of how it was enacted. In Lila's case, there is good potential for a productive discussion of students' engagement in higher order thinking during the lesson. Lila included the text structure study guide as an evidentiary artifact with her lesson plan. Further, her focus question addresses "the application of mystery concepts and vocabulary to a new mystery," which can orient discussion participants toward examining the teaching video for evidence of students' successful classification of clues within the overall text structure of the mystery genre.

Significant Content, Objectives, Artifacts, and Phases of Instruction

Finally, the lesson plan template addresses several elements that might be considered more reflective of a traditional lesson plan. Our interns state the content under study, the learning objectives, and the intended sequence of instruction. They also include artifacts, especially those that demonstrate the effectiveness of the lesson—specifically, evidence of student learning.

Significant Content. Reflective of our commitment to the concept of pedagogical content knowledge and its importance to our approach to teacher preparation, all videoed lessons must be based on significant subject-matter content that is linked to a core literacy practice, the pedagogical component of the lesson. In item 4 of the lesson plan, the intern must state the academic content under study as well as how he or she has thoughtfully organized, structured, and represented that content. Significant content can be defined in a number of different ways—for example, by the Common Core, local district curriculum, or domain-specific knowledge identified by subject-area experts. The transformation of subject matter for teaching occurs as the teacher critically reflects on and interprets the subject matter; finds multiple ways to represent the information as analogies, metaphors, examples, problems, demonstrations, and classroom activities; adapts the material to students' readiness, gender, cultural and linguistic backgrounds, prior knowledge, and preconceptions (those preinstructional informal or nontraditional ideas that students bring to the learning setting); and finally tailors the material to those specific students to whom the information will be taught (Shulman, 1986). When interns view a video for the Instructional Video Assignment, they look for evidence that significant content has been taught and determine whether the lesson builds substantive understandings that students can apply to new learning situations.

In item 4 of the lesson plan template, interns label the various types of knowledge in the lesson. It must be clear, for example, what types of *conceptual knowledge* (for example, ideas, generalization, principles, theories, and models), *procedural knowledge* (such as knowledge of specific types of subject-specific skills and algorisms), and *metacognitive knowledge* (such as strategic knowledge) are conveyed. As was discussed in Chapters 2 and 3, this categorization of knowledge types is based on the Anderson and Krathwohl's (2001) taxonomy table, an important resource that provides interns with the terminology, labels, and language they need to describe clearly the specific categories of knowledge being taught in the lesson. The taxonomy table inculcates the disposition that pedagogical knowledge is inextricably linked with content knowledge as it helps interns unpack the complexity of core literacy practices, which is a fundamental part of decomposing of the lesson so its cognitive complexities can be made more visible to both the students and those watching the video (Grossman, Compton, Igra, Ronfeldt, Shahan, & Williamson, 2009).

Using the taxonomy table to discuss significant content, interns practice a way of thinking about how to structure and represent the content they are directly teaching to students; it helps them distinguish among the various types of pedagogical content knowledge associated with subject-specific strategies and methods that can be used to address students' learning needs in particular classroom circumstances. This is an important consideration for secondary teachers because they don't always include this as part of their instructional responsibilities. An added bonus is that by using the taxonomy table to describe significant content, interns build the repertoire of professional language that we expect them to draw upon during their video discussions (see the trajectory, Chapter 4). In the example of Lila's lesson plan, she does not simply state that her lesson addresses characteristics of mysteries; she states the characteristics in relation to the factual, procedural, and conceptual knowledge that students are expected to draw upon.

Objectives. The objectives serve several functions. As is the case with all objectives, they specifically state what is to be attained in the lesson. Interns' stated objectives must satisfy two criteria: (1) The significant content of the lesson must be identified by both knowledge type (such as facts, concepts, and procedures) and cognitive dimension (interpret, classify, compare, apply, evaluate); and (2) the knowledge type and cognitive dimension must be classified according to the Anderson and Krathwohl (2001) taxonomy table. These are two of the five objectives in Lila's lesson plan:

- Objective 3: Students will be able to categorize characters and clues under mystery-specific classifications (red herring, verbal clue, thematic clue, detective, suspect, witness, and so on). (Type of Knowledge: conceptual—knowledge of classifications and categories; Cognitive Dimension: understand—classifying)
- Objective 5: Students will use evidence from the comic strip to develop logical predictions based on reasoning. (Type of Knowledge: procedural—knowledge of subject-specific skills; Cognitive Dimension: create—generating/hypothesizing)

Objective 3 focuses on the knowledge of classification, a type of conceptual knowledge because it deals with the content of literature. In this particular lesson, it is the specific types of characters that readers find in mysteries—suspects, detectives, and victims. Classifying is an example of the cognitive dimension of "understand." Because the cognitive dimension is understand/classifying, the objective deals with lower order thinking. However, Objective 5 is an example of higher order thinking because it is the cognitive dimension: create/hypothesizing. Objective 5 also focuses on a different type of knowledge: procedural knowledge/the subject-specific skill of developing the logical presentation of evidence. This is an important knowledge type because it deals with the specific skills associated with the literacy strategy being taught in the lesson.

Artifacts. Artifacts (such as a graphic, a handout, copies of PowerPoint slides, questions discussed, or samples of student work) are attached to the lesson (and explained in item 7) for several reasons. They provide concrete evidence of how the core literacy practice is implemented in the lesson, they demonstrate how the literacy activity used in the lesson reflects the characteristics of effective literacy activities, they show how the lesson embodies significant content, and they help viewers better understand how to respond to the focus question. Lila determined that three artifacts would both provide evidence and support discussion participants' understanding of the focus question: (1) the text structure study guide that represented the core literacy practice, (2) the comic strip that served as the text under study, and (3) the posttest that provided assessment information.

Phases of Instruction. The final prompt in the lesson plan template (item 11) directs interns to state the phases of instruction. This sequence describes the flow of the lesson and how the literacy strategy fits into the context of the entire lesson. There are three phases: (1) the beginning of the lesson (that is, how the topic is introduced, how a purpose for learning is set, how prior knowledge is activated, how new vocabulary is introduced, and so forth); (2) the middle of the lesson (how students actively engage in processing the content of the lesson); and (3) the conclusion of the lesson (how the lesson is wrapped up and knowledge learned is summarized and/or synthesized). The inclusion of the entire sequence of the lesson provides important context for the video discussion. To focus the conversation, the presenting intern identifies which phase of the lesson the video represents, as Lila did by noting, "The lesson that takes place in this video clip is a comic strip lesson where students are asked to view/read three sets of panels and apply the vocabulary that we had been learning the past two lessons."

VIDEO SELECTION AND PREPARATION

As has been noted throughout this book, we undertook this project with the assumption that novices' study of videos of their own teaching would be a productive, meaningful experience in terms of their learning to teach. A recent review of research makes it clear that teachers who analyzed their own teaching captured on video found the experience significantly more meaningful than did teachers who analyzed someone else's video (Blomberg, Renkl, Sherin, Borko, & Seidel, 2013). The researchers found that:

> Teachers tended to notice more significant events in terms of relevant components of teaching and learning compared to teachers analyzing other lessons. However, they significantly articulated fewer critical incidents than did those who analyzed another teacher's instruction. (p. 100)

These findings reflect our experience with using video study in secondary content area teacher preparation. Interns' study of their own videos of teaching was productive because of the high degree of personal relevance, which, as the Blomberg et al. research demonstrated, stimulated substantive reflection as well as more in-depth conversation compared to the study of another teacher's video (Blomberg, Renkl, Sherin, Borko, & Seidel, 2013). Interns obviously have deep knowledge of context—including individual students, curriculum, and resources—that contributes to their understanding of what is going on in a recording of their teaching efforts. In addition, when personal videos were used in conjunction with familiar pedagogical strategies (that is, the repeated Instructional Video Assignment with its focus on core literacy practices), learning was enhanced.

In Instructional Video Assignment discussions, interns are, of course, also studying videos of others' teaching as they are shared, along with related focus questions, in small groups. As the Blomberg et al. review—and our own experience—indicates, this study of others' teaching is useful for developing a critical stance toward instruction. Interns were able to identify particular instances and issues in another's video (guided by a well-developed focus question) more readily than in their own videos of teaching. That said, we also found that interns' discussions of teaching were characterized by what might be termed a *culture of nice*: They demonstrated reluctance, particularly in early video discussions, to speak too plainly or critically about another intern's teaching (see Chapter 9 for additional discussion of this issue).

In terms of the practical issues related to creating and preparing a video of teaching, we had very few problems. In the pilot year of implementation of video study, we spent a lot of time on training interns to use video technology and edit videos, which proved largely unnecessary. Our interns, like most people who have even moderate technological literacy, readily use equipment to produce videos of adequate quality for video discussions. The main issue we encountered in the early years was related to the length of the videos. Sharing a full-length video of teaching proved to be both unproductive and impractical. Interns had a hard time attending to critical events, even with a well-designed focus question, in a lengthy teaching video. Further, when so much time was devoted to viewing a single video of teaching, interns had less time to engage in in-depth discussion and had fewer opportunities to share their own teaching. We found that a carefully selected, relatively short video clip, accompanied by the context provided in the lesson plan and a well-designed focus question, was both engaging and productive for participants in the discussion group.

Per the Instructional Video Assignment guidelines, interns are directed to: "Select a 5- to 8-minute video clip of a teaching activity in which you engage your students in learning important disciplinary concepts taught through the careful reading of a text. The video should depict how you use a core literacy practice to strengthen student understanding of curriculum concepts." This idea of selecting a "clip" not only makes the video discussion more focused and manageable, but it also supports individual interns' analysis of and reflection on their teaching as they prepare for the video discussion. Each intern records the full lesson in which the assigned literacy strategy is taught, and must then review the video to determine an appropriate clip and associated focus question for consideration by the discussion group.

With the lesson plan completed and the video clip selected, the interns are ready to discuss their teaching with a small group of peers. Chapter 7 addresses this next stage of the Instructional Video Assignment—the discussion itself.

The Instructional Video Assignment
Part 2—Discussion

> I have learned the value of having evidence to examine after a lesson rather than relying on a feeling or generalized feedback. By videoing, I can go back and prove that something happened or did not happen, if students responded one way or another. Then I can adjust my teaching based on evidence rather than gut feelings.
>
> —Teacher Education Program Graduate

As was explained in Chapter 6, our goal with the Instructional Video Assignment was to create recurring opportunities through the study of videos that would build professional discourse. We envisioned conversations that would help interns identify teacher moves, particularly those representing high leverage practice, and would support the acquisition of a professional skill set for strategic practice. We quickly learned that as potentially rich as a given video of teaching might be, one cannot assume that novices will be able to tap into that richness. Novices need scaffolding and support to engage in productive conversation around that video. Chapter 6 outlined the lesson plan that is part of that support for interns' preparation for video discussion. Here, we address the protocol that guides and structures the conversation as well as the scoring guide that we use to assess the quality of video discussions. We illustrate the use of both of these tools with excerpts from our interns' Instructional Video Assignment discussions.

THE PROTOCOL

We knew, even early on, that we wanted to provide a set of guidelines for how a video-based discussion would proceed. With the lesson plan, and especially the focus question, in place, we developed a series of steps—a protocol—for small groups to follow:

1. *Set the context.* The presenter explains the lesson's background and setting (for example, grade level, content area, lesson objectives, instructional methods).

2. **State the focus question.** The presenter succinctly identifies the problem or issue that he or she would like the group to address.

3. **View the video and restate the focus question.** After the group views the video, the presenter restates the focus question, which is meant to orient the conversation at the outset.

4. **Examine events in the video.** The group analyzes the content of the video, offering evidence from the video to support claims. They address teacher moves, examine events from both teacher and learner perspectives, and identify evidence of characteristics of high leverage practice.

5. **Identify lessons learned.** Interns conclude by stating lessons they learned that could be applied to their own teaching.

Use of this early iteration of a discussion protocol revealed several problems. First, interns largely ignored the lesson plan document, relying on the presenter to provide them with information. The presenter's responses to prompts about the context for instruction, the content under study, and students' responses and reactions were (understandably) usually lacking the detail and coherence of a carefully crafted lesson plan. We wanted interns to attend to the lesson plan document and accompanying documents (such as a graphic organizer used during the lesson) as an initial step in understanding the teaching represented in the video. Second, interns did not always make the connection between the significant content that students needed to learn and the core literacy practice being taught in the lesson. It seemed that interns struggled with what secondary educators have confronted for decades: how to integrate the two seamlessly into what Shulman (1987) and others referred to as pedagogical content knowledge. Third, the focus question and the characteristics of high leverage practice were discussed in a bifurcated manner. Our goal was that the characteristics of high leverage practice would become a filter through which interns examined the focus question and viewed their practice. Instead, interns often approached the characteristics of high leverage practice as a checklist, simply noting the presence or absence of evidence for each in the video. In short, these early video-based discussions too often had a procedural feel as interns simply moved through the steps of the protocol.

As we recognized these recurring issues, we began to revise the protocol based on the curriculum decision-making model. The current iteration, which has three parts, is included as Figure 7.1. Part 1 is designed to set the context for the discussion. This part of the conversation provides the background information needed to interpret the events in the video and elucidates any questions or issues that need clarification. The lesson plan is the focus here: The presenter references key elements of the plan that are pointedly identified in Part 1 (purpose, objectives, artifacts, focus question) in ways that illuminate the connections among them. In Part 2, participants view the video, further address the focus question as well as characteristics of high leverage practice, and reflect on application to their own teaching. In Part 3, interns evaluate the quality of the video discussion. Part 3, which we will not address in depth here, is intended to allow interns and

Figure 7.1. Instructional Video Assignment Discussion Protocol

Select a moderator for the discussion and view the video clip. Make sure each group member has a copy of the protocol before the discussion begins.

Part 1: Before Viewing the Video

1. Begin by reviewing the purpose statement (*why*):
   a. Why did you select the core literacy practice, given the content to be learned in the lesson? Be specific about the connection between the literacy practice and the concepts, generalization, principles, theories, and models of the lesson.
   b. What is the merit? What learning principles underpin the core literacy practice that will help students learn the key content of the lesson?
2. Given the focus of the previous lesson, why does it make sense to use the core literacy practice you selected at this point in the lesson (*when*)?
3. Review the objectives for the lesson.
4. Explain the importance of the artifacts (*how*):
   a. Specifically, how do the artifacts reflect the characteristics of an effective core literacy practice? Explain the connection to each of them.
   b. How does the identified core literacy practice facilitate the learning of meaningful content?
5. Given the purpose of the lesson and the objectives, explain how the formal and informal assessment tasks document what is to be learned in the lesson.
6. Review the focus question:
   a. Does the focus question have both elements (the content focus and the core literacy practice)?
   b. Given the purpose of the lesson, is the focus question appropriate?
   c. Explain the rationale for the focus question.
7. Does the focus question need revising? If so, what are the recommended changes?
8. Given what has been discussed, what do you expect to see on the video?

Part 2: Viewing and Discussing the Video

9. Begin with the focus question:
   a. Unpack the teacher moves observed in the video.
   b. Encourage comments about teacher moves or activities that are relevant to providing feedback on the focus question.
   c. Make specific references to the video and, if necessary, go back and view the video again.
10. Identify elements of teaching practice depicted in the video that represent high leverage practice. If necessary, return to the video and show parts again, if helpful.
11. What are some possible conclusions that we might draw about teaching and learning after viewing this video and talking about it? In what ways can we connect what we discussed about teaching and learning to the theories and principles we've studied so far in your teacher education program?

Figure 7.1. Instructional Video Assignment Discussion Protocol (continued)

12. Talk about what you have learned from this video that you will be able to apply to your practice. (These are ideas that you might use in writing your reflection essay.)

Part 3: Debriefing

13. Debriefing (after discussion of one or two videos):

   a. How would you evaluate the quality of tonight's conversation about teaching practice (for example, how successful were people at citing references to the video to support their observations?)?

   b. Do you think the group reached a shared understanding about the teaching practices discussed tonight?

teacher educators to "debrief" and monitor their progress with engaging in an evidence-based, coherent, and meaningful discussion of practice.

Part 1: Before Viewing the Video

The parts and steps of the protocol are carefully sequenced and aligned with elements of the curriculum decision-making model. We decided to begin the discussion of the video with an explanation of the purpose and the rationale, because it set the stage for introducing several characteristics of high leverage practice (strategic implementation, merit in a variety of contexts, and research and warrant) early in the conversation. By having the presenting intern address the prompts related to purpose, pedagogical content knowledge, merit, and principles (item 1), we addressed the earlier problem of a bifurcated discussion. The characteristics of high leverage practice were integrated at the beginning in a more natural manner by linking them to significant content. In this way, they were less likely to function as a checklist and more likely to be examined as an important filter for guiding and analyzing instruction.

This first part of the protocol is illustrated by one of our video discussions—one that focused on teaching by Emily, who taught 6th-grade ancient world history. Note that this Instructional Video Assignment discussion is not an ideal or perfect example, but rather represents a typical video-based discussion with both strengths and weaknesses. As the discussion began, Emily explained the purpose of the lesson: "to have students use the Claim-Support-Question thinking routine to develop an argument supported by evidence from their textbook and to anticipate counterarguments in preparation for a debate." The statement of purpose in the lesson plan is rather general, but as the context for the lesson unfolded, the intertwining of the literacy strategy with the content under study (the three Chinese philosophies of Confucianism, Daoism, and Legalism) became clearer.

Emily had created a chart intended to support students' engagement in the thinking routine of "Claim, Support, Question." She explained that she wanted students to prepare an argument, and their process of doing so should "mimic the process of thinking that historians do." In the previous lesson, Emily found that students would answer her questions about the Chinese philosophies, but when she asked for evidence, "they kind of just repeat their answer. So I really want to get them to start explaining their reasoning and picking out what from the textbook or from another source made them think that." The purpose of the lesson, Emily explained to the discussion group, was twofold: The thinking routine was used first to ensure that students grasped the key components of Confucianism, Daoism, and Legalism, and second to engage students in constructing arguments the way historians do. She created a chart to help students identify claims about, support for, and questions related to the three philosophies. Use of the chart was intended to scaffold students' engagement in analysis in a way that was consistent with historical inquiry. By aligning the chart with historical inquiry, Emily was attempting to move students from lower order to higher order thinking about the three Chinese philosophies. Her planning efforts demonstrated pedagogical content knowledge, and the modified protocol aided her in making this explicit to the other members of the discussion group.

Another example of how changing Part 1 of the protocol changed the quality of the conversation can be seen in the emphasis on strategic implementation—thorough discussion of *when*, *why*, and *how* the literacy strategy was used for the particular students and content (see items 1, 2, and 4 on the protocol). The explicit attention to strategic implementation is illustrated in Emily's explanation of how she modified the "Claim, Support, Question" thinking routine. Emily had explained that the literacy strategy was chosen with her selected assessment in mind: a debate, which would allow students to draw on their knowledge of and evidence-based thinking about the Chinese philosophies they had studied. Consequently, she had decided to use the "Claim, Support, Question" thinking routine. But she realized that for her purposes, the thinking routine had to be modified to include another level of analysis: a counterargument. As Emily said during the Instructional Video Assignment discussion, "I don't think they've ever really encountered the idea of a counterargument." For the purposes of debate preparation, she wanted to teach her students how to anticipate a counterargument. She added a column on the "Claim, Support, Question" guide she had prepared and then took it a step further—not only did she want students to write a potential counterclaim question, but she wanted them to answer it as well. This illustrates strategic implementation: Emily did not simply insert the use of the "Claim, Support, Question" routine into her lesson; she also modified the chart that represented the thinking routine in relation to her instructional purpose and aligned it with the assessment. Another intern in the group noted that the chart, with this addition, put the parts of the thinking routine "in a step thing from simple to complex kind of work. . . . It connects counterargument [with] argument, thinking about the other side of the perspective to a lot of different things. It has merit in a lot of different situations." The protocol supported Emily in making explicit her strategic implementation of the "Claim, Support,

Question" thinking routine, and the group's recognition of the thinking routine's merit in a variety of contexts.

Changes to Part 1 of the protocol also supported interns in close (rather than perfunctory) examination of the focus question. During the lesson, Emily had modeled the use of a similar chart with the philosophy of Hinduism, which her 6th-graders had studied in the previous unit, to show them how to carry out the thinking routine. Even with this model, she felt her students were not prepared to independently engage in the thinking routine and complete the chart for the Chinese philosophies in preparation for debate. For her focus question, she wondered: "How could I have better introduced the purpose of the thinking routine as it pertained to the three philosophies debate and better modeled for students how to use the thinking routine to prepare an argument for the debate?" This appears at the outset to be a two-part question, seeking feedback first on the introduction of the thinking routine and then on the use of modeling.

During the Instructional Video Assignment discussion, Emily elaborated on the focus question by explaining, "If the purpose of a thinking routine is to help students make their thinking visible and then use that and have it become automatic, I think it'd be difficult for them to do that if they didn't know the purpose of it. I think it's really important that I did a good job introducing it for it to be effective." Dean, another participant, responded, "Yeah. And it seems like you did that; you modeled without necessarily giving the students content that they could possibly use later on and just copy verbatim what you said." Later, responding to the prompt about the focus question's relationship to the lesson's purpose, Emily raised the issue of coherence: "I don't know if I connected the thinking routine with the debate and the three philosophies as best as I could have. I guess [the issue is] tying everything together into a coherent lesson and not just having thinking routine, debate, three philosophies as separate things." As will be seen as the interns began actually discussing the teaching in the video, this statement represents a refinement of what had initially seemed like a two-part focus question: Emily's concern was really about the connection and coherence among three components of the lesson—content (three Chinese philosophies), core literacy practice (use of the chart reflecting the thinking routine), and assessment (the debate).

Emily, as the presenter, spent a good deal of time individually explaining her lesson plan in this portion of the Instructional Video Assignment conversation. Actual discussion—exchanges with other interns that developed ideas—was rather limited. Nonetheless, this typical example illustrates that changes to the protocol led to changes in the interns' approach to the lesson plan during video discussions. The lesson plan was treated not just as a background document but as a text that provided insight into Emily's teaching.

Part 2: Viewing and Discussing the Video

The purpose of Part 2 of the protocol is to guide and structure the discussion based on the video, which can have a tendency to wander and become unfocused.

The interns begin Part 2 by viewing the video. We emphasize note-taking while viewing, including noting time markers at key moments. This allows the group to revisit parts of the video during the discussion to specifically illustrate points, check the accuracy of claims, or get consensus on a claim.

Following the viewing of the video clip, interns revisit the focus question (item 9), which is intended to orient the group's unpacking of the teacher moves and student responses observed in the video. Interns note important observations relevant to answering the focus question; and if necessary, they view relevant portions of the video again. This is the equivalent of engaging in a deep reading of a printed text.

To illustrate Part 2 of the protocol, we continue with the example of Emily's video-based discussion—again, an example that we consider typical and one that illustrates both strengths and weaknesses. The interns watched the video, and then one of the participants, Ben, initiated the conversation:

> You talked about how you could have better introduced the purpose of the thinking routine. I think your big thing was showing a little bit more specificity with the examples that you used. And I think that was the problem with the students. They seemed a little bit lost. Like when you talked about using Hinduism for the debate, I think students were a little bit more engaged and as a result were able to follow. So you probably should have just did a little bit more of those specific examples, I think especially dealing with a middle school population like you were.

Ben's comment—which was actually a suggestion—directly related to the first part of Emily's originally stated focus question, about how she could have "better introduced the purpose of the thinking routine." Ben referenced what he observed in the video, but as his impressions of what occurred ("they seemed a little bit lost," "I think students were a little bit more engaged") rather than as detailed statements of evidence. The other participant, Dean, then picked up the second part of Emily's stated focus question:

> *Dean:* I think the debate of it and the modeling, did you feel that they knew it was going to translate to that? 'Cause I didn't really hear that much of it. I have here at 1:30 you had just finished going through each step of the debate, like the instructions or format. But . . . did you actually say, "Hey, this is how you can use it in the debate. This is how you can use that in debate."
>
> *Emily:* I don't think as much as I should have. . . . I think I could have done a better job making that connection throughout.
>
> *Dean:* Maybe identifying prior knowledge by asking students, "What do you know about debate? What do you know about each step?" . . . I would say that you could use that as a guide to what parts you need to do more of a

job of linking to debate, like why you're going through it just 'cause, okay, that's where they struggle.

Dean addressed Emily's concern about how her modeling the thinking routine with Hinduism, as a previously studied philosophy, could have better supported students' preparation for the debate. He described what he observed in the video, including a mention of a time marker, but again it was not used as evidence, but instead as a point of reference for getting more information from Emily. By drawing on the notion of "prior knowledge," Dean made a suggestion to change Emily's teaching that reflects a research-based characteristic of teaching that he had studied in the teacher education program. These initial exchanges with Ben and Dean represent "answers" to Emily's focus question as required by Part 2 of the protocol, even though they only partially demonstrate the kind of evidence-based, principled conversation we sought.

These exchanges reveal that the interns in this discussion group accepted Emily's premises that (1) her modeling of the thinking routine with a different philosophy was an appropriate approach given the lesson objectives, and (2) her students did not fully understand how to use the thinking routine. These assumptions reflect in part the orientation of Emily's question toward improvement (doing something "better") rather than understanding (examining how events unfolded before moving to suggesting changes). The result is a focus on making suggestions, as is illustrated by Ben's and Dean's comments. The orientation toward improvement is typical for interns, but is not the most productive approach to video discussion. We would have liked to see these assumptions questioned, particularly during Part 2 of the protocol when interns had access to evidence from the video.

A second important function of Part 2 of the protocol is to help identify elements of teaching practice depicted in the video that represent high leverage practice. The illustrations from Emily's video discussion indicated that interns drew upon the characteristics of merit in a variety of contexts, strategic implementation, and higher order thinking. These emerged in a relatively organic way, as they made sense to illuminate the principled underpinnings of Emily's (actual or potential) teaching. This is the kind of natural, sophisticated use of the characteristics of high leverage practice that we hope to see. It is more common, however, for interns to follow the protocol's direction in a checklist-type fashion to discuss each element of high leverage practice in relation to the teaching in the video, as was the case later in Emily's video discussion:

Ben: Significant advances in learning. I wanted to ask you, Emily what do you think they internalized about the content? You said there was a pretty lively debate that was produced based on this. Was that because they really got the content . . . or because they like debating and yelling at each other?

Emily: I think because they like debating it was more engaging. But they
were using their textbooks and using evidence. And they still, like even a
week later yell at each other, like when we were studying the Qin Dynasty.
It's using Legalism and they're like, "See? I told you." And another's like,
"Well, there's going to be a revolt in 10 years."

Ben asked for Emily's impression of what students' engagement in the debate meant in terms of student learning—that is, whether their response indicated significant advances in learning, which was the next element of the protocol.
Emily responded in a relatively evidence-based manner, with an anecdote about
an exchange between students that demonstrates their understanding of content.
Emily went on to explain that the debate "at least made the content . . . a little
more relevant and they still argue points of it. I don't know how sophisticated their
understanding of each philosophy is, but that wasn't really my goal. It was just for
them to know the key components at this point of time in 6th grade." The teaching
represented in the video is in the background here; this exchange, along with the
previous excerpts, illustrates that the video was only one resource in this discussion of Emily's teaching. In video-based discussions, we often find that along with
the video, lesson plan, and selected artifacts, the presenter is a primary resource
that participants frequently draw upon to gather information that sheds light on
the identified focus question.

As interns conclude their discussions, the protocol directs them to think more
generally about teaching and learning (item 11) and the connections to their own
practice (item 12). Although we expect that they will connect research and practice and apply ideas to their own teaching throughout the video discussion, the
inclusion of these items in the protocol gives them an explicit opportunity to do
so. At this point in Emily's video discussion, Ben noted that a "huge" lesson from
Emily's teaching was the idea of "modeling and doing it effectively rather than doing all the thinking" for students. Further, using familiar content to model the use
of the "Claim, Support, Question" thinking routine meant that "at least they had
the knowledge basis to implement [the thinking routine] in territory that they're
unfamiliar with. . . . Then I'd try to hint at it like, 'Okay, we've done this before. Or
we know this.'" Here, Ben picked up on the ideas about the effective use of modeling that emerged during the video discussion. His remarks were punctuated by an
indication of how he might transition students to working independently after he
modeled with familiar content. This is an example of what we hope for as interns
study videos of others' teaching—that they are able to envision principled practice
in the context of their own work as teachers. Ideally, Ben would be able to plan,
implement, and record the modeling he describes in his own use of a thinking
routine with students, and these ideas would reemerge for refinement in a future
video-based discussion.

The revised protocol makes explicit the ways we want video-based discussions to unfold: with careful attention to the lesson plan, associated artifacts,

and the video itself; clarity on the presenter's focus question, which orients the conversation; and attention to the principles that guide practice, especially the characteristics of high leverage practice. The protocol has been an essential tool in enabling interns—relatively independently—to take on and progress with the Instructional Video Assignment, but it is notable that the resulting video-based discussions are complicated and variable. In Emily's example, we saw the complexity of how the focus question was examined and revised, how evidence was used, and how references to principles, including high leverage practice, were embedded. Given this complexity, we have found it necessary to have one more tool that shapes the Instructional Video Assignment—the scoring guide, discussed next.

THE SCORING GUIDE

The final tool that gives structure to the Instructional Video Assignment is the scoring guide that we use to assess the video-based discussions. The scoring guide is used by both teacher educators and interns in at least three ways: (1) to anticipate ways to engage in a high quality conversation prior to discussion, (2) to assess the quality of the discussion and (3) to provide feedback on interns' overall progress toward becoming strategic practitioners.

During the first several years of our work with video discussions, the scoring guide was structured to address the extent to which the discussion examined a connection between the literacy strategy used in the video and the content taught in the lesson, demonstrated a deep understanding of the effectiveness of the literacy strategy to scaffold learning, embedded characteristics of high leverage practice, and resulted in a collectively developed "answer" to the focus question. The scoring guide at this point captured our interest in the connections among the content being taught in the lesson, the literacy strategy, and how both were reflected in the characteristics of high leverage practice. The interns' examination of the focus question represented the intersection of all of these. Throughout the discussion, we wanted interns to use explicit, descriptive professional language in an accurate and confident manner.

Guided by this initial scoring guide, the video-based discussions were positive in many ways. They promoted participation, while building trust among the participants. Interns had opportunities to hear others' voices and perspectives. They were working on solving problems that arose during the discussion about the overall quality of the lesson. They analyzed complex teacher moves, weighed evidence, and made clear and effective suggestions for improving the quality of teaching. That said, as was noted earlier, the discussions also had a procedural feel and did not flow in an integrated, substantive manner. Changing the protocol helped interns move away from this "checklist" approach to video discussions, but we also needed the scoring guide to better define a high quality video discussion.

To construct a scoring guide that aligned with the revised protocol and the trajectory we developed to monitor growth (see Chapter 4), we identified five key indicators of a high quality video-based discussion. The video discussion must: (1) make clear the connection between the significant content knowledge taught in the lesson and the core literacy practice used to facilitate its learning; (2) determine whether the core literacy practice was strategically implemented; (3) analyze and evaluate the implementation of the core practice using the characteristics of the particular core literacy practice as guides; (4) use professional language when discussing the implementation of the core literacy practice; and (5) engage in critical reflection that connects concepts, ideas, and theories embedded in the core literacy practice to research and practice.

The revisions to the scoring guide (see Appendix D) highlight several key changes in emphasis that aligned with the broader curricular changes addressed earlier in this book. First, the revised scoring guide focused on core literacy practices—a narrower category of strategies than had previously been addressed, defined as having utility in fostering the literacy skills of secondary students and forming the foundation for integrating literacy skills into the secondary curriculum. The selection of literacy strategies was no longer determined by serendipity or personal preference; they were a well-defined set that fit with the curriculum decision-making model. Second, the scoring guide emphasized the use of a focus question with two elements: the identification of the significant content to be learned and the selection of a core literacy practice that facilitated the learning of the content. Third, the revised scoring guide introduced the concept of strategic implementation—that is, video-based discussions needed to address not only whether the literacy strategy was used, but also how well it worked. This placed more emphasis on analysis and evaluation. Fourth, professional language was explicitly addressed as a primary emphasis rather than as a background consideration. Fifth, critical reflection was added because of its overall importance in our program and framework.

Using the Scoring Guide

It is important to understand how we used the scoring guide and the type of feedback we provided and how it was aimed at promoting growth along the trajectory as interns progressed toward becoming strategic practitioners. As we studied the work of our interns, we asked ourselves: What does a high quality conversation look like? How does it change over time? How can we make growth tangible and discernible to us and to our interns? We examine these questions as we elaborate on the five traits of our scoring guide and illustrate them with examples from Instructional Video Assignment discussions. We selected these examples to exemplify the essential elements of each trait and demonstrate the areas of growth that characterize movement on the scoring guide. Note that many of the examples illustrate the "Rudimentary" and "Practiced" levels that characterize most interns' video-based discussions by the end of the 1-year teacher education program. We cannot and do not expect that interns will perform at the "Strategic" level in just a single year of teacher preparation. The inclusion of the "Strategic" level (which is explicitly stated at the beginning of each Trait's explanation, below) defines the characteristics of ideal evidence-based discussions of practice that we hope interns will continue to work toward in their early years of teaching.

Trait 1: Connection Between Significant Content and Core Literacy Practice

At the Strategic Level: The core literacy practice is aligned with significant content and is delivered in a seamless and skillful manner that makes the connection between the core literacy practice and the critical content clear to the learner.

This trait addresses how interns make sense of the relationship between the content of the lesson and the core literacy practice, and how these functioned in the context of the lesson. We want interns to discuss how the use of the core literacy practice facilitates learning of the particular content. As sophistication with interpreting the relationship between the two develops, we expect that interns will be able to judge the extent to which the objectives of the lesson were facilitated by the implementation of the literacy strategy.

Consider the following example:

Stacy: So I thought your video was really interesting in that . . . you provided a scenario and asked them, "If you were to envision this as a government, what would it look like?" I thought that was really interesting to get them to think outside the box. Was this a hook for your lesson? Because I think it could definitely function as one. I don't know if that's how you used it.

Juan: It was incorporated into their bell work so I guess by nature of the timing of it, it was somewhat of a hook, yeah. It started out the lesson. It was something for them to do as they walked in. The example was already up on the projector with directions that said, "Talk about this among the people at your table."

Stacy: I think the placement of it within the whole lesson was really nice. And I liked that at around 35 seconds, so right at the beginning, a kid offers his answer and you say, "What do you mean by that?" And you're really giving him the chance to expand. I liked that. I thought that was a good example of high leverage practice.

Notice how this exchange begins. Stacy asked if this was a "hook," or a method used to get a class started; however, it does not qualify as a core literacy practice. The discussion is not oriented by a focus question that addresses significant content and a literacy strategy, and the result is primarily requests for more information ("Was that what you were looking for?") and generic evaluative comments ("I thought it worked well", "I liked that"). Per the scoring guide, this Instructional Video Assignment discussion received an "Unfocused" designation, because the conversation did not address a core literacy strategy and made no connection between the strategy and the content.

In the next example, which we characterize as "Rudimentary" relative to Trait 1, the group did address the focus question (summarized by Allan in his first statement), and they immediately recognized that it lacked clarity and needed revision. This group realized that before they viewed the video, it was important to understand what specific type of feedback that Allan, the presenter, wanted.

> *Allan:* What I'm looking to do is make sure that my instructions are concise enough for all my students because while I had a pretty high level of engagement, not everyone was there, and I wasn't satisfied with the level of engagement that I had. So I'm hoping to see if maybe that's where my lesson kind of needs to be tweaked in order to help get that level that I'm looking for.
>
> *Natalie:* I think that you could be a little more explicit in terms of what aspects of student participation you want more clarity about. I think what you were going for is how you could improve your instructions to get more focused participation in terms of them actually implementing the activity. Does that—am I—
>
> *Allan:* You're on the right track. I'm looking at it in terms of did my instructions help promote a good final product. . . . I know I didn't get explicit enough with my students in saying that you cannot use the word *thing*, you cannot use *something*, you can't use *stuff*. I know for a fact that's one part where we broke down, but I want them to be more concise with their definitions and I think that requires me being more concise with my directions.
>
> *Natalie:* So you're talking more about the product: Did your instructions give them the tools they needed to create the product that you wanted them to have at the end?
>
> *Carlos:* My question is the structure of the word map; is that what you had an issue with, with your graphic organizer?
>
> *Allan:* No. I think the graphic organizer was pretty solid for helping them get to where I wanted them to be. I think it's more maybe the sequence of my instructions or is there some places [sic] where I maybe need to be more explicit than others, and I guess that's really what I'm looking for. I thought that maybe by just modeling it would have achieved that, but clearly that wasn't the case.

The group probed to clarify Allan's initial focus question, which was a somewhat general question about how he gave instructions and the impact this had on student engagement. Natalie suggested that the focus question was addressing the "activity," which Allan then revised to address the "product" that students would create. These comments reoriented Allan's focus question toward his use of the graphic organizer, which was the core literacy practice represented in this video. This revision puts the content under study within reach for the discussion, even though it is not explicitly addressed in this exchange. With the revised focus question, the discussion has the potential to achieve a more integrated perspective on content and pedagogy.

Trait 2: Analysis of the Strategic Implementation of the Core Literacy Practice

At the Strategic Level: There is explicit evidence that the intern can accurately and skillfully explain the *when, why,* and *how* for implementing the core literacy practice and accurately aligning theory with practice. This is done in a thoughtful, articulate, and strategic manner.

Understanding the idea of strategic implementation is challenging, in part because it is a complex interaction among three important learning principles that are integral to the planning and implementation of a lesson: *why* one selects a particular strategy, *when* in the sequence of the lesson it should be taught, and *how* one scaffolds and models it. Strategic implementation distinguishes the skillful practitioner from the struggling novice. We find that, particularly early in our program, interns might be able to explain one of these—*why, when,* or *how*—but very infrequently are they able to capture the interaction among the three or connect to appropriate theories. The following exchange is indicative of early struggles with this component.

The video discussion centered on the focus question: How effective was the employment of the close reading strategy of textbook sections on Christianity and Buddhism in aiding students to form the concept of "religion"? The short but revealing conversation began with Tim, the presenter, stating, "Because students were about to learn about religions like Christianity and ethical systems like Confucianism, this lesson and teaching practice was strategically implemented so that students could conceptualize 'religion' and analyze whether a particular entity fit the criteria for a religion or an ethical system." Here, Tim had identified the *when* aspect of strategic implementation. Another participant, Reggie, then explained:

> I think there was strategic implementation because you move from the reading to specifically Buddhism and Christianity and . . . then you move on to religion in general. So, if you just asked them to just come up with the attributes for religion by looking at [whether] it did not have, for a lack of a better term, "the middle man," in deciding the critical attributes of Buddhism and Christianity, it would have made generalizing to all religions much harder.

This exchange is primarily an explanation of the lesson's sequence. Reggie hinted at the *how* aspect in describing Tim's use of examples before he made generalizations, but Reggie did not make this explicit. The discussion did not fully address strategic implementation or the relationship among the *why, when,* and *how* elements, nor was there identification of appropriate learning principles and theories. The discussion was scored as "Rudimentary" for Trait 2, as these interns had not yet internalized what it meant to strategically align content and literacy strategy in a thoughtful, articulate, and strategic manner.

Trait 3: Evaluation and Analysis of Implementation of the Core Literacy Practice

> *At the Strategic Level:* The evaluation and analysis of the implementation of the core literacy practice is accurate, precise, and demonstrates the ability to improve learning through the systematic implementation of the characteristics of effective core literacy practices.

We added this trait to the scoring guide because we found that although we could identify interns' use of critical thinking in video-based discussions, that thinking often lacked sufficient depth around certain aspects of the lesson—particularly the implementation of core literacy practices. For example, interns using graphic organizers sometimes designed these as note-taking activities focused on copying and transferring information rather than as routines for stimulating deeper thinking about significant subject matter, scaffolding learning, and fostering higher order thinking. We wanted interns in video-based discussions to question whether this was occurring and to consider revisions that would make the use of a graphic organizer align with the characteristics of high leverage practice. To support this, we provided a list of Characteristics of Effective Graphic Organizers (see Figure 2.2). We provided similar lists tailored for each of the five core literacy practices.

The following excerpt illustrates some of the specificity and attention to principles that we sought in Trait 3. In this exchange, interns began with a clear explanation of a graphic organizer and then shifted to a more detailed critique of why it was problematic. Notice that the comments are not generic but are specifically centered on what is needed to make effective use of the graphic organizer.

Lila: So how does this graphic organizer reflect the characteristics of an effective graphic organizer?

Drew: I feel like each of the questions in the graphic organizer move from basically factual knowledge. So the first question here for each document is: Who wrote it, when, and what type of sources? That's basically factual knowledge about the source itself. And then the next segments are sort of, what's the tone? It's kind of asking the students to make inferences. . . .

Like how does this soldier feel about what happened in the battle? So basically I would say it moves from factual to making inferences in this graphic organizer.

Lila: The last box asks, "Is this source trustworthy and why?" That's higher order thinking. That's "Evaluate, Critique, Judge," whether someone's perspective is trustworthy or valued, or should be valued. [But] everybody [represented in the student work samples] is saying yes.

Drew: Right.

Lila: In my thinking, if I were reading these, I would be like, "This person is too personally connected to this. They can't really look at it without bias." So maybe you need to talk a little bit more about what bias is.

Lila specifically used the language of the Anderson and Krathwohl (2001) thinking taxonomy to analyze the questions on the graphic organizer as she remarked, "That's 'Evaluate, Critique, Judge.'" Then her comments shifted to examining the student artifacts, which included the completed graphic organizer, and concluded that students were having difficulty determining bias, which meant the graphic organizer could be improved to function more appropriately. The interns analyzed and evaluated both the design and implementation of the graphic organizer, addressing the characteristics of an effective graphic organizer and seeking to move students to a deeper understanding of content by scaffolding higher order thinking. This discussion was scored as "Practiced" for Trait 3, but the specificity of the recommendations approach the "Strategic" level.

Trait 4: Use of Professional Language

At the Strategic Level: Professional language is used concisely and accurately to describe the implementation of the core literacy practice; it is used with depth and specificity that foster the development of a dialogue that builds a professional community by connecting theory and practice.

Professional conversation necessarily encompasses professional language. Professions, including teaching, have agreed-upon definitions that are essential to having meaningful conversations (for example, scaffolding, modeling, higher order thinking). We want novices' conversations about teaching to reflect the discourse of a professional community. We want to support them in using professional language accurately, clearly, and concisely to communicate and refine ideas about practice and to avoid misunderstanding or misconceptions. In video-based discussions, the use of professional language supports interns in seeing and naming connections among their experiences, and in making connections to concepts and ideas they learned in coursework. We found that making professional language an explicit aspect rather than a background variable in the scoring guide helped both interns and teacher educators work on its improvement.

In this example, Sara posed her focus question: Did my use of the graphic organizer as a supplement to my lecture help my students better understand economic systems? Sara expressed concern that her graphic organizer had functioned simply as, in her words, "a glorified note-taking sheet," which was not what she had in mind. She went on to note that she was "worried" about it, which led to the following exchange between Sara and Jamal, another intern:

> *Jamal:* You said you're worried. What makes you worried about it?
> *Sara:* I guess I was worried that I didn't do enough scaffolding from the simple to complex. I did add those questions at the end because I didn't see a way to move [students] to complex thinking just using the boxes and the arrows, but the graphic organizer part itself and the questions feel kind of like an afterthought. . . . I guess I'm just wondering if there would have been a better way to use it or a better time to use it or a better way to develop the actual graphic organizer itself.

Sara clarified her concern about the graphic organizer, and the perspective she wanted her peers to take as they studied her video, by using professional language. She referenced the use of scaffolding and movement from simple to complex understandings—both key elements of the use of a graphic organizer as a core literacy practice. This use of professional language supported Sara in communicating analytical thinking about her use of the graphic organizer as she struggled with how to move students from one level of thinking to the next.

After watching the video, the interns in this discussion revisited Sara's focus question and began addressing particular moments that they believed provided insight into the question. Jamal described a point at which Sara had referenced the graphic organizer to ask students a question during her lecture:

> *Jamal:* It seemed like your question at 2:40 [minutes] of, "Any ideas why this [economic system] might be the most common?" moves them into applying what they've just talked about in relation to the system. It also made me wonder if there was an opportunity for them to—it was hard to hear, so maybe you did—but justify their answers with evidence. I don't know what kind of text you had—
> *Sara:* We were discussing real-world examples for each economic system.
> *Jamal:* Does it connect to prior information that they have learned about related economic systems, that you could say, "Based on what we just talked about in the previous lessons what makes this the most common?"
> *Sara:* In relation to that question, no, not specifically. This is kind of all the new material. I could have connected it back to [the three questions] I introduced at the beginning: "How it's produced, who it's produced for, and what is produced?" . . . because we had been talking about the factors

of production in the previous lesson, and that's really what you need to produce. I guess I could have connected it back to that more to get some strategic implementation in there.

In this exchange, Jamal addressed the idea of using the graphic organizer in the context of the lesson to build connections between the new content being presented and what students already knew. First, he saw connections between aspects of the content presented during this lesson, and second, he suggested there could be connections with content learned in previous lessons. Jamal's remarks evoked several concepts that these interns studied in the teacher education program—including prior knowledge, coherence, and cohesion—but he did not use these terms explicitly. Using professional language to capture these concepts might have led to elaboration on how and why making the connections Jamal suggested would benefit students' learning in this case. It might also have moved this exchange from the particular realm of Sara's teaching to support the application of those concepts within each intern's own teaching context.

This video discussion was scored at the "Rudimentary" level for Trait 4. Although there were moments (as in the first exchange) in which professional language was used clearly, accurately, and in a manner that fostered the development of dialogue, there were also some missed opportunities (including the second exchange) for using professional language.

Trait 5: Use of Critical Reflection in Relationship to Core Literacy Practice

At the Strategic Level: Reflections demonstrate a critical, in-depth ability to connect concepts, ideas, and theories in the strategic implementation of the characteristics of effective learning. Several insightful, detailed examples for improving the lesson are offered as well the inclusion of reflections that lead to action.

We want interns to engage in critical reflection so they can make meaning of their experiences by synthesizing evidence gained through video study and applying what they learned to their future teaching practice. When interns reflect critically, they look beneath the surface to see what influences their behaviors, resulting in increased depth of understanding about practice. In addition, critical reflection enables them to step back from particular events and view their teaching more holistically. This enables interns to expand their understanding of experiences so they are better equipped to manage similar future situations (Thompson & Thompson, 2008). According to Mezirow (1990), "Perhaps even more central to adult learning than elaborating established meaning schemes is the process of reflecting back on prior learning to determine whether what we have learned is justified under present circumstances" (p. 5). In this view, critical reflection is a precursor to transformative learning: It can lead to changes in both personal understandings and potential behaviors through the transmutation of thinking about presuppositions that sometimes constrain the way interns perceive, understand, and feel about practice. Critical reflection can change past perceptions and thinking, which in turn leads to new understandings about one's practice (Gardner, 2009; Smith, 2011; van Woerkom, 2010).

To support critical reflection, we asked interns in video discussions to speculate about alternative approaches and future implications based on their conversation about the particular events represented in the presenting intern's video. Item 12 in the protocol asks interns to apply ideas from the video-based discussion to their own practice. We want them to consider: What would you do differently next time? Why? What are the lessons learned (such as an idea, product, process, or concept) that could be shared with your colleagues? In this way, critical reflection encouraged the integration of theory and practice while enhancing student learning and self-confidence. The challenge for us as teacher educators was to support the interns in engaging in this complex process.

The following exchange about a world language lesson, which received an "Unfocused" designation for Trait 5, illustrates a lack of critical reflection:

> *Chanita:* So I think I learned . . . I need to be more explicit in my instruction
> about what I want to see from [students] and my expectations about
> what I want from whatever they're thinking. Could be more wait time,
> giving more time to generate their thoughts, maybe accessing previous
> knowledge before I do this activity since it was previous vocabulary. Give
> them some time to think about it before I ask them to reproduce it. And
> then what I'll apply to my practice, I think what I just said. I'm going to
> apply that to my practice.
>
> *Toni:* And this is just something also I noticed in general. I notice you talk
> pretty quickly, and this is a second-year class, right? So you might want to
> think about repeating more or speaking a little more slowly.

Here, the presenting intern mechanically listed several ideas from the discussion as representing what she learned. At best, she appeared to be answering a question from the protocol without indicating the relevance of what she has learned to her future practice or the way she thinks about teaching and learning. This is not the critically reflective thinking we seek; the discussion did not address the ways these suggestions for refining teaching were linked to principles of learning. In short, there were no insights that could lead to transformation of practice.

In a second example, Jackie, the presenting intern, reflected on the effectiveness of her use of a core literacy practice—a "See, Think, Wonder" study guide she developed to support students' analysis of political cartoons. In this exchange, Chet began by referencing a time marker from the video as evidence that students were truly engaged with and learning from the activity:

Chet: At 6 minutes [into the video] when they're talking about Uncle Sam being drunk or disoriented from all the policy changes, I think that shows they're really getting into the content and really learning a lot from the experience of using a graphic organizer.

Jackie: The very last thing that the video ends on is one of the students looking at it going, "If you look at Uncle Sam, his eyes just look crazy and he looks like he's looking at FDR with this look in his eye of, 'Oh my God, what are you going to do to me now or what are you going to do to me next?'" I feel like prior to that none of the students were looking at those little details and making the connections. . . . I actually felt like finally we had established a good enough routine that they could look at political cartoons and take something away from them.

Chet: I'm looking back at your objectives and the third one is, "Students will be able to understand that opinions of FDR varied and [for] what reasons." To make that even more like higher level thinking it could say "Critique them." Say like, "We do a lot of work with political cartoons in our class and we always have to try to understand the author's perspective." That was at the root of your focus question. And like the fact that there were different perspectives on it, so they could critique it and say how much they agree or disagree with the author's perspective to take it a step further.

Jackie: I have political cartoons that I'm going to be using for World War II. And I plan on using "See, Think, Wonder" because I think they've got that routine down. And I definitely think I'll add that question about the author's perspective.

Between them, Jackie and Chet established that the lesson was effective in supporting students' analysis of the political cartoon. Jackie indicated that students had acquired a new sophistication for examining visual information and would apply it to future learning experiences. She attributed this effectiveness to the "routine" established through use of "See, Think, and Wonder" with the accompanying graphic organizer. It was evident from her comments that she would use this core literacy practice with the modification of Chet's suggested question about author's perspective. This discussion received a "Rudimentary" designation for Trait 5. There was clear indication of critical reflection that led to new understandings about, and potentially change in, Jackie's practice; however, the group did not address broader concepts, ideas, or theories that could extend these insights beyond the context of Jackie's next lessons involving political cartoons.

CONCLUSION

In this chapter and Chapter 6, we described the process we used in designing supports for discussions of video records of practice and the tool we used to assess interns' growth on their path to being strategic practitioners. The last task in the Instructional Video Assignment is for interns to write a reflection about what they have learned from their experience in creating and discussing a video record of practice. In the next chapter, we will discuss not only the reflection task that concludes the Instructional Video Assignment, but also the Reflective Writing Task that our interns use to build their understanding and expertise in critical reflection on the work of teaching.

CHAPTER 8

Transforming Teaching

Reflecting on Video Records of Practice

Ultimately, we want interns' efforts to learn teaching through the study of videos of their practice to be transformative; that is, we want the experience to change (and improve) the actual work they do in classrooms. In this chapter, we elaborate on critical reflection as the process by which ideas and insights developed in video-based discussions are positioned as changes to novices' practice. We describe two carefully structured assignments that are intended to engage interns in critical reflection on insights gained through their study of videos and other records of practice. First, we address the final component of the Instructional Video Assignment—a written reflection that is designed to elicit interns' reflection on what they have learned from planning, enacting, and discussing video records of practice and how they will change their current practice to incorporate what they have learned. Second, we examine an additional video-based assignment that is designed to increase our interns' skill in reflecting on their practice and that of others for the purpose of transforming their practice: the Reflective Writing Task.

ROLE OF CRITICAL REFLECTION

Critical reflection is used to deepen and expand interns' insights into their own practice as well as the practice of others. The idea of critical reflection is introduced in the Instructional Video Assignment discussions and formalized in the reflective essay (described below) that interns write following these discussions. In the Reflective Writing Task assignment, critical reflection is taken to another level: It becomes an intellectual responsibility. For us, reflection is a thread that is pulled through the program and woven into the fabric of courses and assignments. Critical reflection is an indispensable component in the development of intellectual character and manifests itself in the form of strategic practice. Understanding the learning process does not happen merely through experience alone but rather as a result of thinking about or reflecting on what is being learned. From Dewey's (1933) perspective, knowledge, desire, and attitude work together to produce a general disposition of thoughtfulness, one of the elements of which is reflective thinking. Reflecting on teaching is a way of grounding the learning experience for interns and is, therefore, more than a recollection of what happened or what was done. When reflections are no more than reports of events, they serve little purpose. As Stanton (1990) noted, when reflection on experience is weak, students' "learning" may be "haphazard, accidental, and superficial" (p. 185). For us, reflection is more than just thought: It embodies critical analysis and evaluation founded on the criteria and standards for effective practice. Therefore, it must engage interns in thinking about their teaching in a way that will help them improve in the future.

When activities are designed to enhance critical reflection, as the Instructional Video Assignment and Reflective Writing Task are, they promote significant learning. In these assignments, reflection acts as a way of organizing knowledge about one's human experiences. It is through reflection that one acquires abstract knowledge. We want interns to form abstractions about the practice of teaching and be able to implement them in very concrete and practical ways. Understanding the abstractions and theories that form the foundations of strategic teaching practice is necessary if interns are to pull out the intellectual work of teaching for more careful examination. When critical reflection is thought of in this way, it becomes transformative because it promotes deeper insights into practice. Critical reflection and strategic teaching are inextricably linked because critical reflection produces strategic action. In the following sections, we describe how we use critical reflection in video-based assignments.

REFLECTING ON INSTRUCTIONAL VIDEOS

We emphasize critical reflection at the conclusion of the Instructional Video Assignment because of its potential to move interns "beyond a knowledge base of discrete skills to a stage where they integrate and modify skills to fit specific contexts" (Larrivee, 2000, p. 294), and therefore toward strategic practice. We depend on the transformative nature of critical reflection to aid interns as they use interpretations of their experiences to guide their future actions (Mezirow, 1990). In other words, reflection is an essential component of the Instructional Video Assignment because it leads interns to modify their practice based on what has been learned through the critical analysis and evaluation of a teaching experience depicted on video so that it can be carefully examined.

For example, in the following excerpt from her Instructional Video Assignment reflection, an intern talks about what she learned and how she will adapt her next lesson. The intern had used a thinking routine to launch a lesson on South African folklore. After viewing and discussing the videos of her colleagues, she realized that she had not provided sufficient purpose for the thinking routine and, therefore, had not achieved her objectives as well as she expected. Below is her analysis of how she used the core literacy practice (the thinking routine) and how she planned to adapt it in the future.

Different from Risa, Dan, and Eric, I chose to use the thinking routine as the jumping-off point for my lesson on South African folklore. Because my students had performed this routine once before, I did not spend as much time talking about how to do the routine. Additionally, I did not discuss the purpose and importance of the routine, in that it would serve as the way in which they would learn to think more critically about cultural influences on mythology. By the end of the lesson, via formative assessments like the gallery walk, whole-group discussion, and quick writes, I saw that students were thinking deeply about how the environment influences the values of a group of people. The main objective for the lesson was accomplished, but I think that I could have been more explicit in explaining how we are using thinking routines to challenge our thinking and develop hypotheses. Without purpose, the thinking routine is just a routine to students.

When looking over student work, I noticed that there were several students making sophisticated connections based on their observations. However, I also noticed that many students were making surface-level connections, and some that were not related to cultural values and folklore. In his lesson, Dan included a slide at the beginning of the lesson where he discussed what he noticed in the previous lesson and made suggestions for how to improve in this lesson, and he included a slide that stated the objectives for the day, one with the essential question, and one that stated the purpose of that day's activities. These slides make Dan's thinking visible to students, and made explicit the expectations that Dan had for that lesson. I think that I could have improved my lesson by including an objective slide, a purpose of the lesson slide, and most definitely an essential question slide. Perhaps if students were thinking about the essential question, "How are cultural values and beliefs reflected by mythology and folklore?" they would have been able to make more specific connections to culture and folklore in the "See, Think, Wonder" routine.

In her reflection, the intern used her experience and those of her colleagues to analyze how well she had enacted the core literacy practice and to plan future enactments. She moved beyond critical reflection to transformation of her teaching practice, stating explicitly what she learned from her and her colleague's enactment of thinking routines and how she will change the way she presents a thinking routine in the future.

The quality of interns' reflection in the Instructional Video Assignment improves throughout the program. At the beginning of the program, interns' skill in reflection is rudimentary, often simply a recap of the teaching experience. We found it necessary to provide direct instruction in how to engage in critical reflection before we saw movement from superficial discussion of practice to the in-depth analysis that leads to transformation. The next section discusses the purpose and format of an assignment designed to increase our interns' skill in critical reflection.

THE REFLECTIVE WRITING TASK

Well before technology made video study readily accessible, we emphasized reflection as an essential aspect of transforming practice. We learned over the years that our interns' idea of "reflection" resulted too often in retelling and superficial personal responses to an event, so we designed an assignment to increase interns' skill in critical reflection: the Reflective Writing Task. This assignment, which recurs five times across the 1-year program, helps interns integrate what they are learning by synthesizing the design principles upon which the program is built. As video study took a central role in our program, the nature of evidence used within the Reflective Writing Task changed to include more evidence of interns' actual teaching, but the assignment's purpose—to promote the kinds of critical reflection that leads to changes in teaching—has remained the same.

Structure of the Reflective Writing Task

The structure of the Reflective Writing Task leads interns through a formal process that requires them to unpack the practice they are analyzing, connect it to educational theory and provide a rationale for why the theory is appropriate, evaluate the quality of implementation of the practice, and explain how the practice can be improved in the future. In order to successfully complete the task, the interns need a framework for evaluating effective practice; therefore, we link the analysis to our program's standards and benchmarks for effective teaching, which describe the knowledge, skills, and dispositions of teaching. In the Reflective Writing Task, video records of practice, as well as other rich teaching artifacts, are carefully selected by interns to provide compelling evidence of their understanding of the standards and benchmarks. This information is used to analyze and evaluate interns' enactment of complex teacher moves, to document their growth over time, to improve the depth and quality of their ability to reflect critically on their practice, and to develop the professional language that facilitates communication among peers and professionals affiliated with the program.

Each Reflective Writing Task is focused on a different standard or combination of standards and is collected over the course of the program. The Reflective Writing Tasks are structured in a way that allows interns to provide evidence of their understanding of the program's standards and benchmarks by answering an essential question. This essential question provides a context for interns to offer evidence of how the standards and benchmarks are reflected in their own practice. Further, focus questions provide interns with the opportunity to delve deeper into the knowledge, skills, and dispositions of teaching. This is accomplished through the use of video records of practice and other teaching artifacts that help students think about their own practice by unpacking the complex moves of teaching that are captured in the examples proffered. This, in turn, becomes the documentation for the progress they are making as their understandings of the intricacies of teaching evolve over the course of the program through the orchestrated critical reflections that form the basis of the assignment.

The format of the Reflective Writing Task is straightforward (see Appendix E for the full assignment guidelines). The Reflective Writing Task begins with an introduction in which the intern provides an overview of the claims that will be addressed in response to the essential question identified as the topic of the Reflective Writing Task (for example, What have you learned about preparation and planning for instruction and how can those insights be applied to your own teaching? What have you learned about classroom environment and how can those insights be applied to your own teaching?). These questions are patterned after those advocated by Wiggins and McTighe (2005) and provide a larger context that creates a frame for thinking about the standards and benchmarks, becoming a catalyst for reflecting on important issues related to teaching practices. The essential question for each Reflective Writing Task is used to determine the degree and extent to which interns comprehend the standards and benchmarks and can provide evidence of their depth of understanding.

The body of the Reflective Writing Task requires interns to provide evidence that they understand each of the benchmarks listed under the standard that is the topic of the Reflective Writing Task, and the body of the response is rigidly structured to ensure that interns address the elements of critical analysis. For each benchmark addressed, interns identify records of practice that serve as evidence of their understanding of a particular benchmark and explain how the records of practice illustrate the content of the benchmark (a claim). Next, interns analyze and evaluate their enactment of the core literacy practice and other core teaching practices and provide warrant for using the practice to achieve their objectives. Finally, interns discuss how they will improve their enactment of the core literacy practice and other core teaching practices for use in the near future. They repeat this structure (description, analysis/evaluation, lessons learned/application) three to five times as they demonstrate their understanding of each of the benchmarks listed under a standard.

The Reflective Writing Task concludes with a reflection on what interns have learned about their teaching relative to the standards and benchmarks. This part contains thoughtful and insightful reflections that demonstrate an understanding of the essential question and its connection to how what is learned can be applied in a clear and concise manner to one's own teaching. This is accomplished through the examination of teacher moves and then by scrutinizing records of practice critically to gain a deeper understanding of the knowledge, skills, and dispositions of teaching by making connections to research and practice.

Example of an Early Attempt at Reflection

The following is an excerpt from a Reflective Writing Task written by a world language intern early in the program. He explains in his introduction that the topic of this Reflective Writing Task is "Preparation and Planning for Instruction" (Standard 1), and the focus question is: "What have you learned about preparation and planning for instruction and how can what you have learned be applied to your own teaching?" The first artifact he presents is a video clip of part of a lesson that depicts him introducing an anticipation guide to his students and the discussion that followed.

Illustration/Explanation

The artifact shows me introducing an anticipation guide to the students and the discussion that ensues. The students were to read a text called *Der Chiemsee*, which is about the Chiemsee, a lake and popular tourist destination in southern Germany. The students had never completed an anticipation guide, so I was transparent in my explanation of its purpose and goals. The students then made their predictions about the text. The clip shows the students' presentation of their predictions and the debates that occurred among students with varying opinions. Prior to reading the text, the students had been introduced to *das Imperfect*, the imperfect tense in German. Although the text includes and requires knowledge of this grammar construct, the focus of the lesson was to bring students to higher order thinking and an understanding of a piece of culture, the Chiemsee.

Analysis/Evaluation

Benchmark 1.3, Build on Prior Knowledge: In this artifact is demonstrated how I require students to make predictions about a text about a lake in Germany. They make these predictions based on what they already know about lakes, tourism, and German geography. This prior knowledge is, by way of the predictions and class discussion that ensues, connected to information gleaned through reading the text. Some students' notions about lakes and tourism proved not as immutable as they had thought once they learned that, for instance, the Chiemsee is indeed visited in the winter by many tourists and that a castle is in fact located at its center. One might say that by implementing the anticipation guide I increased the considerateness of the text *Der Chiemsee*. According to Bonnie Armbruster,

> Considerate texts also address incorrect prior knowledge that readers may bring to the text. Misconceptions can be very resistant to change. Therefore, the authors of considerate texts seriously consider readers' ways of thinking. They try to overcome problems with incorrect prior knowledge by refuting common misconceptions. (1996, p. 55)

Had the students not made predictions prior to reading the text, they might not have even been aware of the preconceived notions they had held.

Benchmark 1.8, Scaffolding and Modeling Instructional Activities: The video clip shows the second part of this competency—namely, that students think in complex ways about course content. After implementing the anticipation guide during the lesson, however, I had students complete a text preview, which activated their prior knowledge. They were to recall the meaning of words that would appear in the text. One could say I addressed this competency in a convoluted fashion, beginning first with higher order thinking, then implementing activities that required lower order thinking. The anticipation guide made students hypothesize about course content, while the preview made them recall course content.

Benchmark 1.9, Incorporate Suitable Resources and a Variety of Participation Structures: Shown in this artifact is a quasi–Socratic seminar; the text in question is of no great literary import, nor are the students even discussing what they learned from the text. Rather, they are discussing what they believe to be the content of the text. Nonetheless, a series of small debates ensues and what makes the discussion similar to a Socratic seminar is that, even though there are right answers, as is revealed upon reading the text, the goal of the discussions is not to come to the right answers, but rather to have an opinion, justify it, and learn from the opinions of others.

Lessons Learned/Application
Although I incorporated into the lesson activities that require both lower and higher order thinking, I cannot provide evidence of scaffolding. Moreover, the activity that required higher order thinking preceded that which required lower order thinking. In the future, I should ensure that the activities truly complement each other and that they are sequenced in such a way that students progress from lower order thinking to higher order thinking.

   In my opinion, the discussions that arose from the anticipation guide were extraordinary. In light of the nature of the text—a purely informational text that lends itself to no interpretation—I am amazed that such debates were able to occur. Perhaps I misunderstand the meaning and purpose of a Socratic seminar, but I believe that, given the nonliterary text, the class came as close as it could to taking part in a high quality Socratic seminar.

This example demonstrates an intern's early attempt at critical reflection on his teaching practice. In the Illustration/Explanation section, the intern helps the reader understand the context in which his video record of practice was collected, but he does not connect the video to a focus question or to the role that the core literacy practice plays in meeting his objectives for the lesson. In fact, he fails to identify the core literacy practice that he employs to increase his students' understanding of the text he assigns them to read. What this intern does is not unusual; he focuses on the events in the video, discrete activities that are not fully connected to a conceptual understanding of the work of teaching.

The intern makes several claims in the Analysis/Evaluation section that demonstrate not only his developing understanding of the benchmarks, but also some misconceptions about the meaning of the benchmarks. When he talks about Benchmark 1.3: Build on Prior Knowledge, he makes the claim that making predictions helped expose his students' misconceptions and provided warrant for the value of identifying misconceptions by citing the work of Armbruster (1996) on considerate text. His comments provide evidence that he is developing an understanding of Benchmark 1.3 and using it to plan lessons. However, in his discussion of Benchmark 1.8: Scaffolding and Modeling Instructional Activities and Benchmark 1.9: Incorporate Suitable Resources and a Variety of Participation Structures, the intern seems confused and appears to make contradictory statements: "Shown in this artifact is a quasi-Socratic seminar; the text in question is of no great literary import, nor are the students even discussing what they learned from the text. Rather, they are discussing what they believe to be the content of the text." His analysis and evaluation do not provide sufficient evidence that he understands the connection between the core literacy practice and the anticipation and preview guide that he used in the lesson. He does not appear to be thinking about the higher levels of abstraction that provide justification for the importance of building on prior knowledge, identifying misconceptions and attending to the structure of text in relation to the core literacy practice of teaching with text.

In the Lessons Learned/Application section of his reflection, the intern acknowledges that he may have misunderstandings, but he also realizes that he did not demonstrate that his selection of literacy activities provided scaffolding as he intended. He demonstrates a developing understanding of the benchmarks as well as confusion. In this early stage of learning the work of teaching, he is trying to weave what he is learning together to present a critical analysis (claim, evidence, and warrant), but is faulting when he tries to make significant connections between what he is learning about practice and the foundational knowledge of the field of education.

PROVIDING FEEDBACK TO INTERNS

When providing feedback to interns on their reflections, we focus on supporting their skill in making claims, identifying evidence, and providing warrant. Evidence refers to the video records of practice and other rich teaching artifacts that support the claims made by interns in their reflection. The evidence must be applied consistently and accurately. In essence, this means interns must be clear about the purpose of the evidence and how it substantiates their claims. Interns also need to provide warrant or justification for the claim they make in their reflection. Interns must construct a bridge between claims they make about their understanding of the standards and benchmarks and then produce evidence that supports those claims, the verity of which is not in doubt. In some ways, their written responses to these assignments represent a logical argument, the center of which is the use of video records of practice and other rich teaching artifacts. We expect interns to create a logical connection among all the components of their arguments. This means that in their written responses they are expected to make assertions about their understanding of the standards and benchmarks, claims for which they must offer proof. They must then offer a warrant that is explicit and that explains the connection between the claim and evidence.

There are other considerations as well. First, does the intern apply evidence in a strategic manner? This is important, because we want interns to mount a logical argument explaining why these documents support their claims. Second, does the intern use high quality evidence? Along with claim, evidence, and warrant must come a concern for the quality of the evidence proffered. Above all, we want interns to use high quality evidence in a skillful and accurate manner. It is not sufficient merely to cite evidence; rather, the evidence must demonstrate merit and explicitly and directly prove worth. This is important because it requires interns to explain why their evidence is relevant. Requiring this step allows us to discern the accuracy, clarity, and appropriateness of any particular body of evidence and to determine why it should count as support for a claim. Often, this part is left tacit.

The following example demonstrates how an intern builds support for his claims through the use of warrant. In this example, the intern focuses on the Illustration/Explanation phase of reflection, describing the records of practice that have been selected to represent a benchmark—in this case, Benchmark 4.1: Development of Intellectual Character, which specifically states: "The teacher creates and maintains a learning community in which intellectual character is fostered and developed and where individual differences and strengths are promoted by engaging in dispositional thinking." The intern describes a homework assignment that illustrates what he believes is an example of how to build intellectual character in the classroom by centering instructional activities on the significant and meaningful content of his discipline. In this case, it is the concept of Jacksonian Democracy.

> The Jacksonian Democracy homework forces students to critically think on their own about their particular stance on a variety of issues from the course readings. The assignment and class discussion display how I chose activities that develop students' intellectual character and dispositional thinking. Based on Ritchhart's chapter "Rethinking Smart: The Idea of Intellectual Character" dispositions of curiosity, metacognition, truth seeking, open-mindedness and skepticism are all achieved through the Jacksonian Democracy activity (Ritchhart, 2004, pp. 27–31).
>
> For the assignment, the students were forced to closely examine their readings in order to justify their stance on given statements. The

students were extremely responsive and knowledgeable on this homework assignment given that the strength of their argument on their opinion was being graded. Due to the positive response with the activity and through my questioning of some of the students, curiosity was shown as they actively sought new information on the topics in order to strengthen their own argument. Furthermore, truth seeking and metacognition were displayed in the activity during class because students were asked how and why they came to such opinions after they stated their stance. Through this process students were forced to think about how they form a historic argument and differentiate between information to establish what amounts to historic understanding. Once the students took their stance on the given statements and explained their opinions, they initiated a group discussion on the differing viewpoints and were allowed to change their position. Within the discussion some students shifted their position, revealing open-mindedness to new ideas, while others argued vehemently on varying opinions, revealing a degree of skepticism.

This example exhibits how well the intern demonstrates a clear understanding of the benchmark by elaborating on its meaning and by explicitly and clearly connecting the video clip he attaches to the assignment and to other rich records of practice. He begins this section of the Reflective Writing Task by explaining how the homework assignment helped students think critically about the issues raised in the readings his students were assigned. He points out how these primary source materials were an essential component in building intellectual character.

He then goes on to explain how articles he read in his literacy class about intellectual character provided warrant for their inclusion in the lesson. More specifically, the video showed students discussing the survey they completed and captured the exchange among students as they discussed their responses. This was further supported by the inclusion of the survey that students completed, which served as the impetus for the conversation that was captured on the video. This was clearly an elaboration of the meaning of the benchmark and was done in a clear and concise manner. This also provided warrant for his claim. He further supported his understanding of the benchmark by providing an example of the assignment, an attached artifact. He even referenced conversations he had with some of his students about the methods he used in the lesson, which further documented the depth of his understanding.

CONCLUSION

In this chapter, we have examined the importance of critical reflection in novices' video-based study of teaching to promote transformation of practice. We emphasized the importance of providing explicit instruction and guidance in developing their capacity to reflect critically, and we presented a model for an assignment that builds critical reflection skills. By requiring critical reflection on what has been learned and how it will impact interns' future teaching, we build novices' capacity to become strategic practitioners.

CHAPTER 9

Lessons Learned

Over the previous eight chapters, we have asserted that videos of novices' teaching are particularly powerful tools for learning to teach core literacy practices. We have described the curricular framework and the carefully crafted instructional setting in which they are situated. We have elaborated on the nature of thinking and discussion about core literacy practices that video study helps to elicit, and we have illustrated how novices might develop these as they engage in video study over time. In this chapter, we address four "lessons learned" that emerged as we reflected on and wrote about our work with integrating video study as a key component of the teacher education curriculum.

LESSON #1: DEVELOP A THEORETICAL FRAMEWORK THAT SITUATES THE USE OF VIDEOS AND RECORDS OF PRACTICE AS AN ESSENTIAL COMPONENT OF, NOT A SUPPLEMENT TO, HIGH QUALITY TEACHER PREPARATION

As we described earlier in this book, we began the process of incorporating the use of video and records of practice with an overall notion of engaging in "practice-based" teacher education. We initially approached the use of video study as a way of extending our existing curricular framework, which was primarily defined by a set of standards and benchmarks. As we began to grapple with what a high quality video-based discussion of teaching would look like, we found it necessary to explicate what it means to engage in practice-based teacher education. We began with the enhanced framework, with its attention to representation, decomposition, approximation, and documentation, to clarify the purposes and desired outcomes of integrating the study of videos and other records of practice as essential components of teacher preparation.

Use of the enhanced framework led to elaboration of the curriculum decision-making model, which clearly and explicitly makes visible the design principles, foundational precepts, and critical core content at the heart of our teacher education program. The curriculum decision-making model has proven particularly beneficial for systematically resolving differences related to curricular decisions when there are disagreements or multiple options to pursue: It is a way of winnowing and sifting to make coherent, principled curricular decisions. The curriculum decision-making model became the standard we used to judge the appropriateness of potential changes to the curriculum. With the use of videos and records of practice and the emphasis on core literacy practices included as components of the curriculum decision-making model, we are able to consider how these elements should function in relation to the other aspects of the curricular design. The result is that the use of videos and other records of practice to study core literacy practices is integral, not supplemental, to our teacher education curriculum.

With the enhanced framework's emphasis on documentation, we developed another key component that framed interns' work with videos of their teaching: a trajectory that described novices' movement toward becoming strategic practitioners. The trajectory was predicated on threshold concepts that reflect the foundational precepts (enhanced framework, core practices, intellectual character) and essential content (standards and benchmarks, thinking taxonomy) in our curriculum decision-making model. Initially, our feedback on assignments involving records of practice was assignment- and course-focused, which provided little feedback on how interns' performance in video-based discussions was indicative of their development as teachers and users of core literacy practices. Using the trajectory allows us as teacher educators to understand interns' progress along a continuum of professional growth, and to set goals to further that progress. The trajectory is a tool for novices as well, providing a "roadmap" to guide them through their evolving understanding of what it means to be a strategic practitioner. The trajectory moved our understanding of quality to another level: We have a way to trace novices' development of competencies, including their use of core literacy practices, as they move through the teacher education program.

LESSON #2: PROVIDE A SET OF SUCCINCT, ALIGNED TOOLS TO SUPPORT NOVICES' ENGAGEMENT IN STUDYING CORE LITERACY PRACTICES THROUGH VIDEOS AND OTHER RECORDS OF PRACTICE

Here, we use the word *tool* to represent both the concrete artifacts and the specific frameworks for thinking that we provided to interns to support their study of videos and other records of practice. Early in the process of incorporating video study into the program, we expected that interns would discuss videos of teaching with ease, given the potential richness of the artifacts and their high interest in sharing their own teaching. We provided simple tools to outline expectations and procedures. These proved to be inadequate support for the complex work of discussing videos of one's own and other novices' teaching.

In terms of concrete tools, consider what we provide to interns for the Instructional Video Assignment: assignment guidelines that outline procedures and expectations, the protocol that shapes their discussion, and the scoring guide used to determine quality. These three tools are aligned to provide interns with a clear sense of how to prepare for the assignment and engage in a high quality discussion and how they will recognize success.

Because the tools carry the weight of shaping the video discussion, they are detailed. The protocol, for instance, outlines numerous elements that are part of a 20-minute Instructional Video Assignment discussion. The simple protocol we had initially developed did not support interns' understanding of the context needed to interpret events in the video, formation of a clear and engaging focus question that would guide examination of the core literacy practice, or use of professional language that would allow for connections among ideas and across experiences in the teacher education program. The current iteration of the protocol includes prompts that require deep consideration of the lesson plan (including probing lesson purpose) and interpretation of the focus question before the video is viewed. After viewing the video, interns are directed to develop responses to the focus question, with claims and warrants supported by evidence from the video. Finally, the protocol directs interns to reflect on lessons learned and the application to their own practice. The protocol and associated tools are designed to support interns' relative independence with selecting a video, formulating a focus question, engaging in meaningful discussion around the video, and making principled connections among experiences.

In addition to developing concrete tools, we provide "thinking tools" that have proven essential for interns' effective study of videos of their own and other novices' practice around core literacy practices. The characteristics of high leverage practice are one such tool, which enables the interns to hone their use of core literacy practices over time. In the context of video-based discussions of teaching, the characteristics of high leverage practice aid interns in determining how a core literacy practice functions in a particular context and the quality of the lesson's enactment. The characteristics represent professional language that supports connections across teaching experiences.

Anderson and Krathwohl's (2001) thinking taxonomy is another thinking tool. Novices frequently struggle with how to decompose the knowledge and cognitive complexities of core literacy practices. The thinking taxonomy provides explicit language and succinct definitions that are useful for unpacking the knowledge, skills, procedures, and complex thinking upon which core literacy practices are predicated. Recurring use of the thinking taxonomy helps the interns think in a deeper, more principled manner about their practice and discuss the enactment of the core literacy practices in professional language.

LESSON #3: TEACH NOVICES HOW TO REFLECT CRITICALLY AND USE PROFESSIONAL LANGUAGE AS ESSENTIAL PARTS OF THEIR STUDY OF VIDEOS AND OTHER RECORDS OF PRACTICE

One theme in this book is that videos are seductive: They are exciting, potentially rich representations of teaching that many of us expect will naturally elicit deep discussion of important ideas about practice. Our experience shows that this is not necessarily the case. Novices need explicit teaching, practice, and support to engage in effective video study—to be able to reflect critically on and engage in meaningful, professional conversation about their teaching.

Video study is a useful vehicle for supporting critical reflection, as interns can revisit events multiple times, taking various perspectives. It is difficult for novices to recognize the thinking and motivations that underlie particular instances of their teaching, but doing so helps them develop a more comprehensive understanding of the complexity of practice. Before interns embark on the Instructional Video Assignment, we extensively model and rehearse critical reflection relative to videos of teaching. We engage interns in increasingly complex analysis of practice as we systematically deepen their understanding of the process of making claims, presenting evidence, and providing warrant. Then they engage in reflecting critically during the recurring Instructional Video Assignment, which is carefully structured to elicit alternative approaches and applications to future teaching.

Critical reflection goes hand in hand with professional language. We have emphasized that video-based discussions of the use of core literacy practices should reflect the discourse of a professional community. The use of professional language supports novices in naming connections among their experiences and making connections to concepts and ideas they learned in coursework. Novices should progress in using professional language accurately, clearly, and concisely to communicate and refine ideas about practice and to avoid misunderstanding or misconceptions. Already, we have described the tools we use (that is, characteristics of high leverage practice and thinking taxonomy) to support interns' use of professional language. These were key elements of the curriculum development model and aligned with the learning trajectory. The professional language represented in these tools was not simply jargon; it enabled interns to talk, think, act, and perform like a strategic practitioner. We asked interns to engage with these tools repeatedly so that the concepts and ideas they represent would become part of their professional language.

Importantly, we have found that nurturing development of both of these elements—critical reflection and professional language—is key to overcoming the "culture of nice" that characterizes some video discussions among novices. Particularly early in the process of sharing and discussing videos of their teaching, our interns focus on complimenting what they perceive as positive in the teaching they observe (for example, "I like the strategy you used," "The students seem really engaged"). These early discussions lack depth; novices at this stage do not question their own or their peers' instructional choices or assumptions. As they gain facility with critical reflection and professional language, they are more likely to look beyond the surface of the teaching represented in the video—to recognize the enactment of principles, question instructional decisions, and examine suggested changes in relation to their own instruction.

LESSON #4: ATTEND TO, BUT DON'T GET
MIRED IN, THE PRACTICAL CONSIDERATIONS

We have learned many lessons about the "nuts and bolts" or the practical consid-erations involved in using video records of practice to support novices' learning of core literacy practices. We grappled with puzzles such as the ideal length for a video, the size and makeup of discussion groups, the benefits and challenges of teacher educator–led versus intern-led discussions, and the appropriate length for discussions.

Frankly, there are no perfect solutions to these kinds of issues. We made de-cisions based on trial and error, asking the kinds of questions that all teachers do: What configurations best enabled interns to meet our objectives? How could we disperse our limited resources (such as screens, projectors, instructional spaces, and teacher educators) equitably? What could be accomplished in the amount of time we had? In general, we found that using smaller groups of novices (three to four) who teach the same subject area results in more productive conversations. These small groups are necessarily intern-led, given the number of groups, with teacher educators rotating among them, observing and offering support as they see fit. We also found that using short (5–8 minutes) videos alongside the lesson plan and the focus question, within a 20-minute time frame, enables more targeted, coherent discussions. Limiting the time for each video discussion usually allows all members of a given group to share their videos in a single session, which can support interns' recognition of themes and concepts that emerge across discus-sions. We suggest that these are simply guidelines that you might use as a starting point for your own work; as with any instructional innovation, you make decisions based on your objectives, students, and resources. Try to anticipate the practical requirements, establish clear guidelines, and then make adjustments as needed.

CONCLUSION

This book has addressed our efforts to use video study to support novices' learn-ing of six core literacy practices. Over 10 years of this work, we have watched our interns grow in their ability to effectively use these core literacy practices to support their students' learning of content, and we have heard from our graduates that their facility with using core literacy practices has paid dividends in their first years of teaching. We attribute these successes in large part to the fact that our interns were able to use video to methodically study and adapt their use of these strategies. They did so in the company of their peers, with an eye toward the goal of becoming strategic practitioners. As we stated at the outset, we are convinced that novices' engagement in studying records, and especially videos, of their practice is essential to their learning to teach. We hope our efforts, captured in this book, contribute to our field's efforts to create a practice-based curriculum that prepares novices to reach every student from their first days in the classroom.

Effective Teaching Standards and Benchmarks

STANDARD 1: Planning and Preparing for Instruction

Benchmark 1.1—Significant Content. The teacher identifies and selects significant content (e.g., facts, concepts, generalizations, and theories) for units and lessons within units that are derived from department, district, and state curricula. This content is the basis for objectives, activities, and assessments.

Benchmark 1.2—Challenging Learning Goals and Objectives. The teacher creates challenging learning goals and objectives that reflect the wide range of learning needs of students and instructional purposes; they are stated in explicit cognitive language (e.g., identify, interpret, compare, exemplify, apply, analyze, and evaluate) and are measurable.

Benchmark 1.3—Prior Knowledge. The teacher creates activities within and across lessons that build on and activate students' prior knowledge (i.e., factual, conceptual, procedural, metacognitive) by connecting new ideas and concepts to already familiar ideas.

Benchmark 1.4—Range of Abilities. A teacher creates lessons that take into consideration a range in student abilities within each class with regard to such factors as types of knowledge (e.g., factual, conceptual, procedural, metacognitive), cognitive dimensions (e.g., remember, interpret, exemplify, synthesize, apply, analyze, and evaluate), developmental differences, and learning needs.

Benchmark 1.5—Diverse Backgrounds, Experiences, and Interests. The teacher creates lessons within each unit that reflect the diverse backgrounds, experiences, and interests of students by considering such factors as race, gender, sexual orientation, religious preference, and life experiences.

Benchmark 1.6—Motivation to Learn. The teacher creates lessons and units that engage students in individual and cooperative learning activities that help them develop the motivation to achieve by such activities as relating lessons to students' personal interests, allowing students to have choices in their learning, and leading students to ask questions and pursue problems that are meaningful to them.

Benchmark 1.7—Sequencing Lessons and Activities within Units. The teacher sequences the lessons and activities within lessons and the unit so they reflect a clearly logical progression (beginning, middle, and end) that provides evidence of alignment among the goals, objectives, lessons, and activities.

Benchmark 1.8—Scaffolding and Modeling of Instructional Activities. The teacher creates a variety of instructional strategies (e.g., lecture, lab, inquiry, group work, discussions) within and across the lessons of the unit and devises ways to monitor their effectiveness.

Benchmark 1.9—Suitable Resources. The teacher includes suitable resources to engage students during the lessons and activities that are aligned with instructional goals and objectives, student interests, and literacy levels.

Benchmark 1.10—Technology. The teacher integrates meaningful use of technology into planning and preparation, and uses it as a tool to enhance student learning ensuring that technology-based activities are engaging, age-appropriate, and based on accurate, significant, and worthwhile content.

STANDARD 2: Designing and Using a Variety of Assessments

Benchmark 2.1—Alignment of Assessment Tasks. The teacher uses backward design to align assessment tasks with curricular goals and objectives that reflect various types of knowledge and cognitive dimensions.

Benchmark 2.2—Variety of Assessment. The teacher uses a variety of assessment formats (e.g., true/false, multiple choice, short answer, essay) and assessment types (projects, presentations, observation, discussion) at frequent intervals during a unit of study to monitor and evaluate student learning.

Benchmark 2.3—Informing Instruction. The teacher uses information from a variety of assessments (e.g., formative and summative, individual and group, formal and informal) at a variety of levels (classroom, district, state, and national) to design instruction that results in improved performance for all students and reduces gaps among demographic groups.

Benchmark 2.4—Maintaining and Sharing Information. The teacher maintains useful records of student work and performance and communicates student progress knowledgeably and responsibly, based on appropriate indicators, to students, parents, and other colleagues.

Benchmark 2.5—Specific and Timely Feedback. The teacher provides specific and timely feedback about student performance with sufficient guidance so that students know how to improve the quality of their work.

Benchmark 2.6—Engagement in Self-Assessment. The teacher uses assessment strategies to involve learners in self-assessment activities that help them become self-regulated learners who are able to set and monitor personal learning goals and make adjustments when required.

STANDARD 3: Implementing Instruction

Benchmark 3.1—High Leverage Practice. The teacher uses elements of high leverage practice to engage students in active learning that embodies these elements: has merit in a variety of contexts, has warrant based on research and accepted theory, engages students in substantive learning, develops and implements higher order thinking, results in evidence of significant advances in learning, and demonstrates strategic implementation of an instructional activity or practice.

Benchmark 3.2—Adequate Instructions and Appropriate Language. The teacher gives clear and adequate instructions, uses correct and expressive spoken and written language with well-chosen vocabulary that is appropriate to students' developmental levels, and anticipates possible student misunderstandings.

Benchmark 3.3—Instructional Methods. The teacher uses a variety of instructional methods (e.g., cooperative learning, interactive lectures, demonstrations, guided inquiry, simulation, and role-playing) so that students assume more responsibility for their own learning.

Benchmark 3.4—Discussion Techniques. The teacher uses a variety of discussion techniques (e.g., Socratic seminar and substantive conversation) that deepen subject-area knowledge, encourage critical thinking, and build dialogue that promotes collective understanding.

Benchmark 3.5—Questioning Techniques. The teacher asks high quality questions that: span the various knowledge types and cognitive dimensions, are adapted to the language and ability levels of students, use a purposeful sequence, stimulate a wide range of student participation, probe initial student responses, and make use of appropriate wait time.

Benchmark 3.6—Lesson Presentation and Adjustments During Instruction. The teacher monitors and adjusts the flow of lessons in response to student feedback for the purpose of improving student learning (e.g., altering a task or activity, clarifying directions, summarizing, providing graphic organizers).

Benchmark 3.7—Different Viewpoints, Theories, and Ways of Knowing. The teacher represents and uses different viewpoints, theories, "ways of knowing," and methods of inquiry in the teaching of subject-matter concepts in order to promote the development of critical thinking, problem solving, and performance capabilities.

Benchmark 3.8—Praise and Encouragement. The teacher uses a variety of nonverbal techniques (e.g., eye contact, facial expressions, and body language) and verbal techniques (e.g., affirmation, verbal acknowledgments) with students to praise and encourage them.

STANDARD 4: Creating a Positive Classroom Environment

Benchmark 4.1—Development of Intellectual Character. The teacher creates and maintains a learning community in which intellectual character is fostered and developed and where individual differences and strengths are promoted by engaging in dispositional thinking.

Benchmark 4.2—Safe Learning Environment. The teacher creates and maintains a safe learning environment in which all students are treated fairly and respectfully by establishing clear standards of conduct for all students, monitoring student behavior in a preventive way, and responding to misbehavior in ways that are effective and sensitive to students' individual needs.

Benchmark 4.3—Smoothly Functioning Learning Community. The teacher creates and maintains a smoothly functioning learning community in which students assume responsibility for themselves and one another, participate in decision-making, work collaboratively and independently, and engage in purposeful learning activities in ways that foster deeper understanding through higher order thinking.

Benchmark 4.4—Demonstration of Care and Respect. The teacher demonstrates genuine caring and respect for students by listening and talking to them, building social relationships among students, being sensitive and responsive to clues of distress, investigating situations, and seeking outside help as needed to remedy problems.

Benchmark 4.5—Daily Routines. The teacher creates and maintains daily routines and procedures (e.g., getting into small groups, controlling disruptive behavior, getting the class started, handling materials and supplies, taking attendance) that establish a reliable classroom structure that promotes continuity and consistency in the learning environment while not diminishing student creativity and risk-taking.

STANDARD 5: Relationships Within and Outside of School

Benchmark 5.1—Advocate for Students. The teacher acts as an advocate for students by being proactive in serving students (e.g., finding needed resources, consulting counselors, talking with teachers of other classes and activities within the schools, and contacting professionals in other community agencies).

Benchmark 5.2—Honor Students. The teacher makes a particular effort to challenge negative attitudes and helps to ensure that all students, particularly those traditionally underserved, are honored in the school.

Benchmark 5.3—Working with Colleagues. The teacher participates in collegial activities designed to make the entire school a productive learning environment by collaborating with professional colleagues within the school (e.g., mentor teacher, counselors, administrators) as supports for reflection, problem solving, and new ideas, actively sharing experiences and seeking and giving feedback.

Benchmark 5.4—Parent/Guardian Partnerships. The teacher communicates with parents/guardians frequently and with sensitivity on both positive and negative aspects of student progress for the purpose of establishing respectful and productive partnerships that support the learning and well-being of students.

Benchmark 5.5—Contributions to School. The teacher contributes to school activities (e.g., plays, sports, clubs), promotes school goals, and improves professional practice by working collegially with all school staff.

Instructional Video Assignment Guidelines
Core Literacy Practice: Text-Based Learning

The purpose of the assignment is to capture and discuss an example of your teaching that depicts techniques you use to support your students' learning with and from text. The focus of the video clip should be on the moves that you make to prepare students to engage with using text to develop a conceptual understanding of important disciplinary content. You are required to use a research-based literacy activity (for example, anticipation guides, semantic feature analysis, close reading technique, and pattern guides) to support independent learning from text to reinforce concepts, learn procedural knowledge, or develop vocabulary that helps them make sense of text.

The assignment has four parts:

1. Posting materials: Upload a video clip, lesson plan/description, and artifacts
2. Audio discussion: Audio record and post a small-group discussion in which you and the students in your group discuss videos submitted by each of you using our discussion protocol, which is provided in the assignment
3. In-class discussion led by instructor
4. Reflection: Post a short reflective essay describing what you have learned from viewing and discussing this round of video records of practice

Part 1: The Video, Lesson Plan, and Artifacts

Select a 5- to 8-minute video clip of a teaching activity in which you engage your students in learning important disciplinary concepts taught through the careful reading of a text. The video should depict how you use a high leverage literacy activity to strengthen student understanding of curriculum concepts. When you plan your lesson, incorporate one of the literacy activities that you've read about in your coursework, or researched on the Internet or in professional trade books (such as an anticipation guide, pattern guide, semantic feature analysis, or close reading technique).

The video clip should be accompanied by a lesson plan following the provided template. If you are following your mentor's lesson plan, make sure you have captured it accurately. You may also create your own lesson plan. You should also include handouts and other artifacts that might help those viewing your video clip understand what they are seeing. Note that you will identify a focus question (item 8 of the lesson plan template) to guide the discussion of the video.

Part 2: Audio Recorded, Small-Group Discussions of the Videos

The purpose of Part 2 is to discuss each person's video clip. Each clip will be discussed and recorded separately. We suggest that two people record each discussion segment so that if a problem arises, you will have a backup. The discussion of each video clip should be at least 15 minutes in length and recorded and posted by the person whose video clip is being discussed. You are assigned to a group based on your content area. Each group will have three to four members. In order to make effective use of your discussion time, prepare for each discussion by viewing the video and reading the lesson plan and artifacts prior to the scheduled discussion.

As you read the lesson plan, make sure you understand the context of the lesson, its objectives (especially the objectives associated with the part of the lesson you are viewing), the focus question, and the characteristics of high leverage practice embodied within the lesson. Begin the discussion with what you observed in the video clip. For example, can the focus question be answered, given the content of the lesson viewed? Are the objectives aligned with the content of the lesson? Treat this portion of the discussion as you would a Socratic seminar: connecting what you observed in the video clip (the text) with the focus question. During the discussion, references should be made to specific parts of the video clip that are associated with your comments. Take notes so that you can direct others to view again the section of the video you want to address. This portion of the discussion is about clearly understanding the teaching moves you observed, specifically those related to the focus question. It is not about evaluating the quality of the lesson. In other words, your comments should be substantive and address issues related to the questioning techniques depicted in the video. Once you have addressed the focus question, discuss whether you think the video demonstrates high leverage practice. Make sure you discuss each of the characteristics of high leverage practice. The discussion should conclude with an evaluation of how well you think your group did.

Part 3: In-Class Discussion Led by Instructor

You will participate in a small-group discussion in which you view and discuss one or two videos submitted for this assignment that have been selected by your instructor because they depict topics of interest to a number of you and will lead to a productive discussion about teaching practice in your content area. Although an attempt will be made to view a video submitted by each student sometime during the year, this will not be possible in all groups. Discussion of records of practice in Part 3 of this assignment provides feedback on specific aspects of core literacy practice selected by the instructor.

Part 4: Reflective Essay

After class you will write a short reflective essay about the important lessons you have learned and explain how those lessons can be applied to your own teaching. The reflection should be based on what you learned during the discussion with your colleagues and the discussion led by your instructor. You should talk about what you learned from viewing and discussing the videos of your colleagues as well as what you learned when discussing your video.

There are two parts to the reflective essay. Part 1 is a thoughtful synthesis of the important ideas you derived from viewing and discussing the video clips; it is not a summary of the discussions. In this part of the essay, you offer insightful reflections that demonstrate your understanding of the key ideas that emerged from the discussion of using a literacy activity to learn from text. Part 2 of the reflective essay is an explanation of the lessons learned from the discussion, ones that can be applied to your own teaching. It should be clear from your response just what you took away from the various discussions that you can use in future teaching situations.

Your reflection should contain specific examples from videos and discussions. It should also connect what you have learned to educational theory, and you should make reference to works we have studied in the program using internal reference APA style. Each part of the essay is approximately three-quarters to one page in length.

Characteristics of Effective Literacy Activities Designed to Facilitate Learning with Texts

1. Establishes a purpose for learning the content (a purpose for the lesson).
2. Situates the content within the goals of the broader course curriculum.
3. Builds knowledge of key vocabulary.
4. Moves student thinking from simple to complex (balance between lower order thinking and higher order thinking).
5. Supports the creation or the expansion of schema (guides students to organize knowledge in organized structures and makes connections among facts, definitions, ideas, concepts, principles, procedures).
6. Scaffolds student's learning by activating prior knowledge and teaching skills needed to successfully achieve the outcomes of the lesson.
7. Provides opportunities for students to construct meaning of important knowledge through independent interaction with the lesson's text.

Lila's Lesson Plan

Instructional Video Assignment
Lesson Description

1. What was the purpose of the lesson?

    The purpose of this lesson was to reinforce mystery concepts surrounding vocabulary and text features in a new and authentic context. Students were asked to apply (implement) their knowledge from the last two lessons, and from their prior experiences with mystery novels, in order to analyze (attribute) the features of the comic strip and fill out the guide.

2. What was taught in the previous lesson?

    This lesson is the third in a series of three lessons surrounding features of mystery texts and mystery vocabulary. In the first in the series, students took a pretest on the information, performed a List-Group-Label activity to activate their prior knowledge on the features of a mystery text, and worked together with me to develop a network tree so that they would be able to see the relationships between the "Types of Characters," "Types of Clues," and "Types of Problems" generally found in a mystery. This day focused specifically on the five multiple-choice questions on their pretest, and the second day of lessons focused on the five short-answer definitions they were asked to provide on their pretest of "hunch, motive, alibi, deduce, and testify." On this day, we performed an activity similar to OPIN [a content literacy activity developed by Frank Greene, described in Vacca & Vacca, 2002], where students were asked to fill in the blanks of six sentences with the correct mystery vocabulary word and then justify their answers. More specific information about these activities can be found in the "phases of instruction" near the end of this lesson plan. The activity performed in the lesson in the video clip is a comic strip text analysis accompanied by a study guide that is used to bring together all the information students learned in the last two lessons in a new and authentic context. This activity was meant to reinforce concepts.

3. In what grade level/course was this lesson taught?

    This lesson was taught in 7th-grade English language arts.

4. What concept/idea and other types of knowledge (for example, principles, theories, models, procedures, and strategies) were taught in the lesson?

> **Key Idea:** text features and vocabulary associated with the mystery genre of literature, and how to use them to make claims and predictions when reading a mystery text

> **Strategy:** reading a mystery novel as a problem-solution narrative

> **Procedure:** gathering evidence to formulate a logical conclusion

> **Literary Concepts:** verbal clue, thematic clue, red herring, physical clue, typecast characters (detective, suspect, witness victim)

> **Subject-Specific Vocabulary:** alibi, motive, testify, deduce, and hunch (may have different meanings in various contexts, but what do they mean in a mystery?)

> **Literacy Strategy:** study guide following a problem-solution outline; students use the study guide to aid in independent comprehension and analysis of text features

5. What were the objective/s? In parentheses after the objective/s, identify the specific knowledge level (type and subtype) and cognitive dimension (category and cognitive process) (Anderson & Krathwohl, 2001).

> **Objective 1:** Students will be able to remember mystery vocabulary words. (Factual knowledge, knowledge of terminology) (Remember, recall)

> **Objective 2:** Students will be able to apply mystery vocabulary to new mysteries. (Metacognitive knowledge, strategic knowledge) (Apply, implement)

> **Objective 3:** Students will be able to categorize characters and clues under mystery-specific classifications (for example, red herring, verbal clue, thematic clue, detective, suspect, witness, and so on). (Conceptual knowledge, knowledge of classifications and categories) (Understand, classifying)

> **Objective 4:** Students will understand that the definitions of vocabulary words and the features of text that we discuss are subject-specific/specific to the mystery genre. (Procedural knowledge, knowledge of subject-specific techniques and methods) (Analyze, attribute)

>> **Justification:** The vocabulary words—*motive, alibi, testify,* and *deduce*—have different meanings in different contexts. I am interested in students understanding what these words mean in relation to the mystery genre.

Objective 5: Students will use evidence from the comic strip to develop logical predictions based on reasoning (deduce). (Procedural knowledge, knowledge of subject-specific skills) (Create, generating/hypothesizing) (Understand, inferring)

6. Explain how you document individual student learning.

    On the final day, I administered a posttest. Students were asked to define the same five words in short-answer responses, and the multiple-choice questions were the same as well, but I moved around the answers to ensure that students weren't simply memorizing letters from the first test. The overall results were promising. Out of 60 students, only a few of them received a grade less than 8 out of 10 on the posttest, and those who did receive a grade less than this had been absent for 1 or more days of the lesson.

7. Include any teaching artifacts that are used during the video clip (for example, a graphic, a handout, copies of PowerPoint slides, questions discussed, or samples of student work).

    a. Include a copy of the literacy activity students complete.

    Artifact 1: Study Guide. This artifact is implicated in the focus question because it is the core literacy practice on which this lesson is based. The focus question asks how well this study guide works to reinforce student application of concepts and vocabulary from previous lessons to a new context. Does this document sufficiently scaffold instruction for students of various learning preferences?

    b. How do the other attached artifacts help viewers better understand the focus question and how do they help scaffold instruction?

    Artifact 2: Mystery Comic Strip—"A Disastrous Dinner." This artifact is implicated in the focus question because it is the text on which students are asked to apply the mystery concepts and vocabulary.

    Artifact 3: Mystery Posttest. This artifact is implicated in the focus question because it represents the information that students will be tested on knowing based on this lesson and the two prior lessons. Students need to know this information at the culmination of the comic strip activity.

8. Identify a **focus question** that will serve as a guide for the viewing and discussion of this lesson. The focus question must be directed at what teacher moves you want help with.

    How well does the problem-solution structured study guide work to reinforce student application of mystery concepts and vocabulary to a new mystery (A Disastrous Dinner comic strip)?

9. **Rationale:** Why is the focus question appropriate for the video segment that will be viewed?

Students in my class have been reading mystery novels for the past several weeks. In the first 2 days of this lesson, we covered concepts and vocabulary that are specific to mysteries, and students applied them to their own stories. In this video clip, I give the students a mystery comic that they have never seen before, and they are asked to apply the concepts and vocabulary we have been learning to a new context. I scaffold the lesson by using a study guide that begins by asking students to lay out how the problem, characters, and clues work together in the beginning and the middle of the story, and how each component contributes to the solution. A mystery narrative follows a problem-solution structure, and I used that structure as the outline of the study guide that I provided for them. I'm wondering how well this literacy strategy (the study guide) aids students in applying the information we learned previously to a new context.

a. Describe the context of instruction depicted on your instructional video.

The video clip occurs just after the students and I finished passing out the necessary materials for the lesson. Students would need their portfolios in which they had their mystery materials from the last two lessons, as well as the study guide and two copies of the mystery comic strip panels per group. I purposefully provided two per group of four students because I was facilitating students in cooperating with one another to construct knowledge. The video clip begins with me explaining the study guide to students so they would be aware of the procedure of the lesson as well as how to fill in the guide. I then activate prior knowledge by asking students to give me some sample responses to two or three of the prompts from the guide, and send them off to work in groups to fill out the remainder of the first part. The video shows them working while I am walking around to check on their progress, as well as me bringing the class back together to share some of their predictions.

b. Which objectives are the focus of the video clip?

The video clip specifically focuses on objectives 1–3 and 5, and implicitly includes objective 4. Objective 4 is implicit because I do not directly instruct students that the vocabulary and classifications that they are learning about are subject-specific, but the use of these in a subject-specific way is inherent in the lesson, and when students are using vocabulary or concepts in an incorrect context, I correct them. Objective 4 was addressed more clearly in the first lesson.

10. In what ways does the teaching practice depicted in this lesson represent high leverage practice?

a. Merit in a variety of contexts:

This lesson focuses on literacy strategies that can be used at any grade level and in any discipline. I provide students with a subject-specific text accompanied by a study guide that they are to use in order to organize the information that they gather under subject-specific concepts and vocabulary. This strategy could be used in a history, math, or science class where the teacher provides students with a subject-specific text and a study guide to help them organize the information they are reading. In history, students could be reading a document concerning ideals that support particular government systems while filling out a study guide in which they categorize the information they get under subject-specific categories such as "republic, monarchy, democracy," and so on. Additionally, the lesson focuses around students gathering evidence and formulating a conclusion. This type of procedure has merit in many disciplines, especially math and science. The study guide that I provide for the students follows a problem-solution structure, which applies to a mystery, but would also apply to a math problem (geometry proof), forming a hypothesis in a science class, and even examining a social or political issue (global warming) in a history or science class. The problem-solution structure is one that students work with on a regular basis. Students at this school write persuasive letters on Friday, in which they are asked to make a claim and support that claim based on logical evidence. This mystery lesson reinforces a procedure that the students are already familiar with and gives them the concepts and vocabulary to apply this procedure to another context (mystery narratives). Using a study guide to support student understanding and analysis of a text can be used many times throughout the semester. I could implement this strategy in the 8th-grade class where they are studying historical fiction, and I could implement it for our units on science fiction and realistic fiction. The study guide might follow a compare/contrast or a sequential structure rather than a problem-solution structure, depending on the genre and which structure most makes sense for understanding. Additionally, this lesson was scaffolded in a variety of ways, so as to be accessible to the majority of students. Students were provided with visual representations to support text, they were provided with a guide to move them through understanding and analyzing the text, they were asked to think and share with their peers to construct knowledge together, and they were able to access the teacher as a resource.

b. Warrant based on research and accepted theory:

The lesson is based on literacy strategies outlined by Vacca and Vacca, (2008) which focus on the use of graphic organizers to aid in student comprehension. The study guide provided is warranted by Vacca and Vacca in their chapter "Working Smart: Study Strategies and Guides." Concerning study guides, Vacca and Vacca state, "Because a study guide accompanies reading [unlike a worksheet, which is meant to be completed after reading], it provides instructional support as students need it. Moreover, a well-developed guide not only influences content acquisition but also prompts higher order thinking" (p. 167). I created the study guide for a number of reasons, one of which was to scaffold student learning. At this stage, I felt that my students necessarily needed a guide on which to organize the information they were gleaning from the text. Vacca and Vacca also note that, "Guides help students comprehend texts better than they would if left to their own resources" (p. 167). If students are not sure how to read the text, the study guide gives them clues as to what features of the text are most important to be looking for. The study guide served to reinforce content acquisition, which the students were in the process of acquiring over the last two lessons, and provided instructional support for students who needed to organize their information. Some of my students may have been able to look at the first six panels and know what to look for as evidence to back up their claims. Others needed the study guide to organize their thoughts before being able to make predictions and draw conclusions. Additionally, the study guide followed a problem-solution structure, which Vacca and Vacca state "works equally well with narrative or informational texts to display the central problem in a story or the problem and solution text pattern" (p. 152). Many narratives begin with a problem that comes to a resolution in the end. Mystery stories almost always follow this pattern. Mysteries are based on a problem that the characters in the story attempt to solve, and in the end, the solution/perpetrator is discovered. I outlined the study guide in this manner by asking students in the beginning of the comic to state the problem on which the mystery was based, and to provide evidence and characters who may have caused or contributed to that problem. They are then asked to infer who may have done the act based on evidence. They do this twice, and the end of the worksheet asks them to provide the solution, and what clues made the solution evident. Implicitly, students were asked to answer the problem-solution questions such as "What is the problem? Who has the problem? What is causing the problem? Who is trying to solve the problem?" (Vacca & Vacca, 2008, p. 153). I think in hindsight I could have explicitly asked these questions on the study guide to make the problem-solution pattern more explicit for students. I never directly stated that looking at a mystery as a problem-solution narrative was a purpose of the task.

c. Substantive learning:

   This lesson focuses on concepts that are at the heart of the English language arts discipline. For instance, the Common Core State Standards for 7th grade indicate under Key Ideas and Details that students should be able to "Cite several pieces of textual evidence to support analysis of what the text says explicitly as well as inferences drawn from the text" (CCSS.ELA-Literacy.RL.7.1) and students should be able to "Analyze how particular elements of a story or drama interact (e.g., how setting shapes the characters or plot)" (CCSS.ELA-Literacy.RL.7.3). The first Common Core Standard is indicated in the lesson because students are asked to use the study guide to gather clues in order to make inferences about the importance of those clues, and how the clues will be implicated in the story's solution. Additionally, students are asked to analyze the text using concepts and vocabulary specific to the mystery genre, which leads into the second standard implicated. The study guide asks students to think about how types of characters, clues, and problems interact to shape the course of the mystery. The study guide asks students to indicate clues, characters, and the problem, and predict possible solutions for the problem based on evidence.

d. Higher order thinking:

This lesson focuses on literacy strategies that scaffold student learning from lower order thinking to higher order thinking. At a base level, the study guide asks students to pick out clues and characters that they see. These are "right there" in the text, and if students are working at the lower level, they will recognize mostly physical clues and be able to point out characters and what they do without classifying them. Students are then asked to use their prior knowledge from previous lessons and interactions with mystery texts to classify the information using concepts and vocabulary that are particular to mysteries. This moves students from the lower level of recognizing a clue (factual knowledge) to being able to classify that clue using disciplinary/subject-specific terminology (conceptual knowledge, knowledge of classifications and categories). The lesson in itself is an exercise in students taking the knowledge that they have gleaned in previous lessons and through thinking about the mysteries that they have been reading, to applying that information in a new context (the comic strip). In the lesson students are using the study guide to analyze how the parts of a mystery work together, as well as to analyze a mystery as a problem-solution narrative. The study guide asks students to state the problem, the possible causes of the problem, who has the problem, and who is trying to solve the problem, and use evidence to point to possible solutions of the problem. This is a strategy that can be performed in a variety of contexts, and is performed weekly in our English language arts class.

e. Documentation of significant advances in learning:

I measured student advances in learning through the implementation of a pretest and a posttest. The tests consisted of five short-answer questions in which students were asked to define mystery-related vocabulary, and five multiple-choice questions that centered on the features typical to mysteries. I had students track their growth on a chart where they indicated their percentage of growth between the pre- and posttests, and the majority of students grew 30–50% between tests. There were a few students who were not present for the pretest or for one or more of the lessons, and those were the students who did not experience as much growth. Student advances and learning were also measured through informal providing of answers and explanations in class, as well as through completion of in-class work-sheets and study guides.

f. Strategic implementation:

When: I implemented the comic strip and study guide in the last segment of my 3-day lesson with the students based on a scaffolding decision. The first day, class centered on activating prior knowledge and helping students categorize that knowledge into disciplinary terms. Both the pretest and the List-Group-Label activities activated prior knowledge, and the concept map organized that knowledge into literary terms. For the concept map, students had provided all of the knowledge, and we worked together to move that knowledge into neat categories such as 'thematic clue" or "red herring." The second day focused on vocabulary acquisition of the five mystery terms: *alibi, motive, testify, deduce,* and *hunch.* Whereas on the first day we were speaking about categories of characters, clues, and problems, the second day we focused on specific things that mystery characters either have or do. For instance, a detective will have a hunch whereas a suspect will have a motive or an alibi. We moved from general categories to more specific vocabulary, and the final day it made sense to implement the comic activity where students would be asked to use all of the concepts and vocabulary they have learned and applied to their own stories in a new context. I chose to do this activity before the posttest because I wanted it to act as a review for the test they would take. Additionally, I gave students 5 minutes between the comic strip activity and the posttest to simply look over their pretest.

How: The "how" is based on literacy strategies that I gleaned from the Vacca and Vacca (2008) reading. I thoughtfully and carefully developed the comic strip where I implicitly implemented the vocabulary and concepts students would need to apply. I developed the study guide in order to supplement student learning, aid comprehension, organize their thoughts, and scaffold instruction.

Why: I created this activity for a number of reasons. I wanted to reinforce students working through a text independent of direct instruction. The first 2 days were guided/directed instruction from the teacher, and the final day was meant to be more independent or student-led. Students worked together in their groups to construct knowledge, while I acted more as facilitator than director of instruction. This activity served as a reinforcement of the concepts and vocabulary that they would be asked to recall for the posttest during that same class period. Additionally, the activity asked students to use problem-solving skills and to apply the information they learned to a new context, which moves them from lower order thinking (simply recalling/remembering vocabulary) to higher order thinking (analyzing a text based on its features and organization, creating hypotheses, and applying/ implementing subject-specific concepts and vocabulary in new contexts).

11. Using the phases of instruction listed below, describe the sequence of instruction for teaching the essential content in the lesson. Also identify which phase the video clip is from.

    a. Beginning of the lesson (how the topic is introduced, how a purpose for learning is set, how prior knowledge is activated, how new vocabulary is introduced, and so forth)

This lesson took place over the course of 3 days. The first day, I administered a pretest to see how familiar students already were with the "ingredients of a mystery" (that is, the types of characters, clues, problems) as well as with vocabulary often associated with mysteries. Students, up to this point, had been reading two mystery novels: one in class and one independently. The goal of this sequence of lessons was to provide students with both vocabulary and text structures/features that could be applied to each of their novels. Additionally, I stated at the beginning of my 3 days that I was providing students with this information in order to prepare them for their summative assessment, which includes a section where students are asked to identify clues, characters, and problems that they came across in their stories. Providing this information is meant to help them prepare for their final project in which they might create a new cover for one of their mystery novels, or write a newspaper article, in which they are expected to implement this vocabulary as well.

I reminded students that the purpose of a pretest was to both activate their prior knowledge and give the teacher a sense of where they are and how much guided instruction will be necessary. I was pleased to see, after going through the pretest, that many students were not familiar with the vocabulary I intended to teach. The second part of the lesson asked students to perform a List-Group-Label activity in order to activate their prior knowledge (Vacca & Vacca, 2008, Chapter 3). I asked students to go up to the board and write under "Types of Characters," "Types of Problems," and "Types of Clues" one thing that they believed to be generally and specifically associated with mystery stories. They could use examples from their own mystery novels, mystery television programs or movies, or their knowledge of what mysteries generally involve to list something. As expected, students were able to list quite a few ideas under each category. We then performed the task of categorizing the information the students provided into literary/mystery vocabulary and terms. For instance, if a student wrote "someone who solves the crime," we would classify this character as a detective.

b. Middle of the lesson (how students actively engage in processing the content of the lesson)

During the last portion of our first mystery lesson, I passed out a network tree, or a concept map, labeled "Ingredients of a Mystery" (Vacca & Vacca, 2008, Chapter 5). I asked students to tell me why we might do a concept map together, and they came up with a variety of answers, such as "to help us categorize information," "so that we have all of this information in one place," "to help us see relationships between the information," and so forth. I was concerned that students would not understand why these types of maps are useful, and wanted to make sure that the purpose for using one was set. The superordinate topic was "Ingredients of a Mystery," with branches for "Types of Characters," "Types of Clues," and "Types of Problems." Branching from those branches were mystery terms such as *detective/sleuth* and *thematic clues*. I projected the map onto the board, and asked students to give me the information to put in the map, all the while asking them to justify their input to the class.

The second day of the lesson consisted of going over the answers to the pretest with students, so that they would have a clear idea of where they were and how much they needed to grow. We then performed a matching activity where I passed out a handout consisting of six cartoons with phrases beneath them, such as "The snake has a _____ for giving the rabbit a hug." Students were asked to use the vocabulary from their pretests to fill in the blanks. Here, the correct answer would be "motive," because *motive* is a word that can be clearly associated with mysteries. When students would give answers like "reason," I would ask them which of our mystery vocabulary words also means to have a reason for doing something. I wanted students to know that they are not wrong, but that this is a task that requires the use of specific vocabulary. This activity is similar to OPIN, in that there were a number of sentences and students were asked to work together to come up with the correct term to fill in the blanks. However, the activity was not opinion-based like a typical OPIN, which asks students to fight for their group's opinion and justify the word that they chose. In this case, there was a specific correct answer to be put in the blank, although I did still ask students to justify their responses in order to ensure that they were learning the vocabulary in relation to the mystery genre (Vacca & Vacca, 2008, Chapter 3). This task was used to reinforce concepts that were introduced on the first day and also, for practicality's sake, was meant to be short so that students would have time to read their in-class novels.

c. Conclusion of the lesson (how the lesson is wrapped up and knowledge
   learned is summarized and/or synthesized)

The lesson that takes place in this video clip is a comic strip lesson where
students are asked to view/read three sets of panels and apply the vocabulary that we had been learning the past two lessons. I pass out the first six
panels of a 14-panel comic strip, along with a study guide, in which students are to fill in information and classify that information using the categories we developed during the first lesson. The study guide asked students
to point out clues and characters and classify those characters in mystery
terms (for example, *blue shoe, physical clue, guy with red shirt, suspect*).
Students were then asked to point out the problem on which the mystery
is based in those first six panels, and make a prediction for who committed
the crime. Students worked in groups to fill out the study guide. I gave a
few students a chance to use evidence to provide a justification for why a
particular character may have committed the crime, and then we moved
onto the next six panels.

The study guide asked the students to repeat the same procedure for
the next set of panels. The study guide then asked students to do a series of
fill-in-the-blank phrases in which they were to use the mystery vocabulary
from the previous OPIN similar lesson and indicate the panel in which
they see that concept being used by a particular character. I was doing
a great deal of work to supplement student learning on five vocabulary
words—*hunch, motive, testify, alibi,* and *deduce*—because they have different meanings in different contexts, and because they are words that I asked
students to define in short-answer constructed responses rather than multiple choice. The last question goes along with the last two panels, where
students discover who committed the crime, and they are asked to state
who did it and provide one specific clue that gave the ending away. The
study guide followed a problem-solution structure, so students were in-
clined to read the mystery as problem-solution narrative. The study guide
begins by asking students to think about "What is the problem?" "Who
has the problem?" "What caused the problem?" "Who is trying to solve
the problem?" "What solutions are attempted?" and "What is the result?"
Mysteries tend to follow a problem-solution structure in which there is a
problem that the detective wants to solve, he or she gathers evidence to see
who/what caused the problem, and reasons to deduce a logical conclusion
about how to solve the problem. This activity acted as the culmination of
the unit because it asked students to apply the information that they were
learning in a new context.

Scoring Guide for Instructional Video Assignment

Traits	Unfocused	Rudimentary	Practiced	Strategic
Connection between significant content and core literacy practice • skill of integrating content and pedagogy • significance of content • alignment	Execution of the core literacy practice lacks cohesion, is confused at times, and the connection between the core literacy practice and the significance of the content is weak and unclear to the learner.	Execution of the learning with core literacy practice is cohesive but presented in a procedural manner; the connection between the core literacy practice and the significance of the content is somewhat confused.	The core literacy practice is aligned with significant content and is delivered in an integrated, practiced, and proficient style that makes the connection between the core literacy practice and the critical content clear to the learner.	The core literacy practice is aligned with significant content and is delivered in a seamless and skillful manner that makes the connection between the core literacy practice and the critical content clear to the learner.
Strategic implementation of the core literacy practice • explains the when, why, and how of the implementation of a core literacy practice • connects explanation to appropriate theory	There is little or no visible evidence that the intern understands or can articulate the when, why, and how for selecting the core literacy practice used in the lesson and its connection to an appropriate theory. The explanation lacks specificity in connecting content to the core literacy practice and theory.	There is minimal evidence that the intern understands or can articulate when, how, or why the core literacy practice is chosen or how it is connected to an appropriate theory. The explanation contains minimal specificity in connecting content to the core literacy practice and theory.	There is some evidence that the intern can explicitly, accurately, and confidently address the why, when, and how for implementing the core literacy practice but sometimes confuses the three. The intern can explain in a general way the connection between theory and practice.	There is explicit evidence that the intern can accurately and skillfully explain the when, why, and how for implementing the core literacy practice and accurately aligns theory with practice. This is done in a thoughtful, articulate, and strategic manner.

Traits	Unfocused	Rudimentary	Practiced	Strategic
Evaluation and analysis of implementation of the core literacy practice • Analyzes and judges the fidelity of the implementation of the strategy • Uses appropriate criteria to judge (characteristics of effective core literacy practices—e.g., moves learners to a deeper understanding of content, scaffolds to higher order thinking)	The ability to judge the quality of the implementation of the core literacy practice is lacking, is frequently inaccurate, and is characterized by a lack of analysis and reference to the characteristics of effective core literacy practices.	There is some analysis and/or judgment about the implementation of the core literacy practice, but it is characterized by some inaccuracies and the omission of some of the characteristics of effective core literacy practices.	The evaluation and analysis of the implementation of the core literacy practice is mostly accurate and precise, and the discussion accurately addresses characteristics of effective core literacy practices.	The evaluation and analysis of the implementation of the core literacy practice is accurate, precise, and demonstrates the ability to improve learning through the systematic implementation of the characteristics of effective core literacy practices.
Use of professional language when discussing the core literacy practice • Concise use of professional language • Depth of dialogue	Professional language is used inconsistently and is overly general when describing the core literacy practice; the conversation does not foster the development of dialogue that builds a shared understanding and is done in a manner that does not offer a rationale for the connection between theory and practice.	Professional language is used when describing the core literacy practice but it is not always precise and clear; the conversation begins to foster the development of dialogue that builds a shared understanding and is done in a manner that offers a general description of the connection between theory and practice.	Professional language that is clear and mostly accurate is used to describe the implementation of the core literacy practice; it is used with some depth and in a manner that fosters development of dialogue that builds a professional community by connecting theory and practice.	Professional language is used concisely and accurately to describe the implementation of the core literacy practice; it is used with depth and specificity that foster the development of dialogue that builds a professional community by connecting theory and practice.

Traits	Unfocused	Rudimentary	Practiced	Strategic
Use of critical reflection on the core literacy practice • Depth to critical reflection connected to theory and practice • Insightful, detailed lessons are identified and elaborated upon	Response demonstrates a lack of critical reflection about the implementation of the core literacy practice; there is no clear indication of lessons learned or what specific changes might be made to improve the overall quality of the activity or reflections that lead to action.	Response demonstrates some critical reflection about the implementation of the core literacy practice; only general lessons and/or improvements are offered; it also includes some reflections that lead to action.	Reflections offer critical insights that connect concepts, ideas, and theories in the strategic implementation of the core literacy practice. Several detailed examples of lessons for improving the lesson are offered and/or includes some reflection that lead to action.	Reflections demonstrate a critical, in-depth ability to connect concepts, ideas, and theories in the strategic implementation of the core literacy practice. Several insightful, detailed examples for improving the lesson are offered as well as the inclusion of reflections that lead to action.

Reflective Writing Task Assignment Guidelines

Topic: Preparation and Planning for Instruction (Standard 1)

Overview of the Assignment

This Reflective Writing Task will illustrate, analyze, and reflect on what you are learning about the importance of preparation and planning for instruction. Address this focus question: What have you learned about preparation and planning for instruction, and how can what you have learned be applied to your own teaching? Use the benchmarks from Standard 1: Preparation and Planning for Learning to answer the focus question. Write about all 10 benchmarks from Standard 1.

In answering the focus question, you will use videos and other record of practice to:

1. explain and illustrate what you have learned about the process of planning lessons or units;
2. explain how you used a core literacy practice to teach key disciplinary concepts in a text;
3. analyze and evaluate what is revealed about your understanding of the benchmarks and standard;
4. explain how the videos and other records of practice helped you gain a deeper and richer understanding of the importance of preparation and planning; and
5. reflect on the lessons you have learned and how they can be applied to your own teaching.

Format of Reflective Writing Task

Selection of videos and other records of practice. Carefully select records of practice that provide compelling evidence of your understanding of the standard and benchmarks. You might choose video clips (5 to 8 minutes in length) of your teaching that demonstrate how lessons and units of instruction are planned and then enacted. Examples may also include lesson plans, recordings of planning sessions, post-teaching debriefing sessions with your mentor, handouts related to the core literacy practice implemented, and student work samples that reflect the result of instruction.

Format. There are three parts to the Reflective Writing Task: introduction, body, and conclusion.

> *Part 1: The Introduction.* The introduction provides an overview, making it clear what the focus is. It should include the focus question and a summary of the records of practice that will be used.

> *Part 2: The Body.* The body is the main part of the Reflective Writing Task. The body focuses on records of practice. The discussion of each artifact has three components. The first component illustrates/explains the record. It describes the context in which the record was observed. The second component analyzes/evaluates the record of practice. This is done by examining the elements of the record and the relationship among them, determining how they are connected to educational purposes and judging their overall effectiveness. The third component reflects/applies what you have learned from the record of practice, how what you have learned has changed your view of teaching and learning, and how you will apply what you have learned to your own teaching. Each section should be introduced with a subhead identifying the component.

> *Part 3: The Conclusion.* The last part of your Reflective Writing Task is the conclusion. Here, you will answer the focus question by looking across the examples of the records of practice and synthesizing what you have learned.

References

Airasian, P. W. (2001). *Classroom assessment: Concepts and applications* (4th ed.). Boston, MA: McGraw-Hill.

Alexander, P. A. (1998). The nature of disciplinary and domain learning: The knowledge, interest, and strategic dimensions of learning from subject-matter text. In C. Hynd (Ed.), *Learning from text across conceptual domains* (pp. 263–287). Mahwah, NJ: Erlbaum.

Alvermann, D. (1981). The compensatory effect of graphic organizers on descriptive text. *Journal of Educational Research, 75* (1), 44–48.

Alvermann, D. (1986). Graphic organizers: Cuing devices for comprehending and remembering main ideas. In J. Baumann (Ed.), *Teaching main idea comprehension* (pp. 210–226). Newark, DE: International Reading Association.

American Federation of Teachers. (2000). *Building a profession: Strengthening teacher preparation and induction. A report of the K–16 teacher education task force.* Washington, DC: Author.

American Federation of Teachers. (2012). *Raising the bar: Alignment and elevating teacher preparation and the teaching profession.* A report of the American Federation of Teachers. Washington, DC: Teacher Preparation Task Force.

Anderson, L. W., & Krathwohl, D. R. (2001). *A taxonomy for learning, teaching, and assessing: A revision of Bloom's taxonomy of educational objectives* (Abridged ed.). New York, NY: Longman Publishers.

Armbruster, B. B. (1996). Considerate texts. In D. Lapp, J. Flood, & N. Farnan (Eds.), *Content area reading and learning: Instructional strategies* (2nd ed.; pp. 47–57). Boston, MA: Allyn & Bacon.

Ball, D. L. (2011, June). *A common core for the training of teachers.* Paper presented at the Science and Mathematics Teacher Imperative National Conference, Portland, OR.

Ball, D. L., & Cohen, D. K. (1999). Developing practice, developing practitioners: Toward a practice-based theory of professional education. In L. Darling-Hammond & G. Sykes (Eds.), *Teaching as the learning profession: Handbook of policy and practice* (pp. 3–32). San Francisco, CA: Jossey-Bass.

Ball, D. L., & Forzani, F. M. (2010). What does it take to make a teacher? *Phi Delta Kappan, 92*(2), 8–12.

Ball, D. L., & Forzani, F. M. (2010/2011). Teaching skillful teaching. *Educational Leadership, 68*(4), 40–45.

Ball, D. L., Sleep, L., Boerst, T., & Bass, H. (2009). Combining the development of practice and the practice of development in teacher education. *Elementary School Journal, 109*(5), 458–474.

Blomberg, G., Renkl, A., Sherin, M. G., Borko, H., & Seidel, T. (2013). Research-based heuristics for using video in preservice teacher education. *Journal for Educational Research Online, 1,* 90–114.

Bloom, B. S. (1956). *Taxonomy of educational objectives, Handbook 1: The cognitive domain.* New York, NY: David McKay Co. Inc.

Boerst, T., Sleep, L., Ball, D. L., & Bass, H. (2011). Preparing teachers to lead mathematics discussions. *Teachers College Record, 113*(12), 2844–2877.

Borko, H., & Putnam, R. (1996). Learning to teach. In D. C. Berliner & R. C. Calfee (Eds.), *Handbook of educational psychology* (pp. 673–708). New York, NY: Macmillan.

Bransford, J. D. (1979). *Human cognition: Learning, understanding, and remembering.* Belmont, CA: Wadsworth.

Bransford, J. D., Brown, A. L., & Cocking, R. R. (1999). *How people learn: Brain, mind, experience, and school.* Washington, DC: National Academy Press.

Bruner, J. (1977). *The process of education.* Cambridge, MA: Harvard University Press.

Carroll, D. (2007). Caring for students while gatekeeping for the profession: The student coordinator role. In D. Carroll, H. Featherstone, J. Featherstone, S. Feiman-Nemser, & D. Roosevelt (Eds.), *Transforming teacher education* (pp. 33–50). Cambridge, MA: Harvard Education Press.

Cohen, D., Raudenbush, S., & Ball, D. L. (2003). Resources, instruction, and research. *Educational Evaluation and Policy Analysis, 25*(2), 119–142.

Conrad, D., & Hedin, D. (1990). Learning from service: Experience is the best teacher—or is it? In J. Kendall & Associates (Eds.), *Combining service and learning* (pp. 87–98). Raleigh, NC: National Society for Internships and Experiential Education.

Council of Chief State School Officers. (1992). *Model standards for beginning teacher, licensing, assessment, and development: A resource for state dialogue.* Washington, DC: Interstate New Teacher Assessment and Support Consortium.

Dalal, D. K., Hakel, M. D., Sliter, M. T., & Kirkendall, S. R. (2012). Analysis of a rubric for assessing depth of classroom reflections. *International Journal of ePortfolio, 2*(1), 75–85.

Danielson, C. (2007). *Enhancing professional practice: A framework for teaching.* Alexandria, VA: Association for Supervision and Curriculum Development.

Darling-Hammond, L. (2000). How teacher education matters. *Journal of Teacher Education, 51,* 166–173.

Davies, P., & Mangan, J. (2007). Threshold concepts and the integration of understanding in economics. *Studies in Higher Education, 32*(6), 711–726.

DeSanctis, G., & Poole, M. S. (1994). Capturing the complexity in advanced technology use: Adaptive structuration theory. *Organization Science, 5*(2), 121–147.

Dewey, J. (1933). *How we think: A restatement of the relation of reflective thinking to the educative process.* New York, NY: D.C. Heath and Company.

Dillon, J. T. (1984). Research on questioning and discussion. *Educational Leadership, 42,* 50–56.

Dreier, O. (2003). Learning in personal trajectories of participation. In N. Stephenson, H. L. Radtke, R. J. Jorna, & H. J. Stam (Eds.), *Theoretical psychology: Critical contributions* (pp. 20–29). Concord, Ontario, Canada: Captus University.

Ennis, R. H. (1987). A taxonomy of critical thinking dispositions and abilities. In J. B. Baron & R. J. Sternberg (Eds.), *Teaching thinking skills: Theory and practice* (pp. 9–26). New York, NY: Freeman.

Eyler, J., & Giles, D. E. (1999). *Where's the learning in service learning?* San Francisco, CA: Jossey-Bass.

Eyler, J., Giles, D. E., & Schmiede, A. (1996). *A practitioner's guide to reflection in service-learning.* Nashville, TN: Vanderbilt University.

Feiman-Nemser, S. (2001). From preparation to practice: Designing a continuum to strengthen and sustain practice. *Teachers College Record, 103*, 1013–1055.

Feiman-Nemser, S. (2007). Professional standards as interpretive space. In D. Carroll, H. Featherstone, J. Featherstone, S. Feiman-Nemser, & D. Roosevelt (Eds.), *Transforming teacher education* (pp. 51–68). Cambridge, MA: Harvard Education Press.

Franke, M., Grossman, P., Hatch, T., Richert, A., & Schultz, K. (2006, April). *Using representations of practice in teacher education.* Paper presented at the annual meeting of the American Educational Research Association, San Francisco, CA.

Frayer, D. A. (1971). *Variables in concept learning: Task variables.* Madison, WI: Wisconsin Research and Development Center for Cognitive Learning.

Frederiksen, J. R., & Collins, A. (1989). A systems approach to educational testing. *Educational Researcher, 18*, 27–32.

Fusco, E. (2012). *Effective questioning strategies in the classroom: A step-by-step approach to engaged thinking and learning, K–8.* New York, NY: Teachers College Press.

Gage, N. L. (1968). An analytical approach to research on instructional methods. *Journal of Experimental Education, 37*(1), 119–125.

Gardner, F. (2009). Affirming values: Using critical reflection to explore meaning and professional practice. *Reflective Practice, 10*(2), 179–190.

Grossman, P., Barker, L., & Brown, M. (2012, February). *Making high leverage practices in secondary English language arts the focus of methods courses.* Paper presented at the annual meeting of the American Association of Colleges for Teacher Education, Chicago, IL.

Grossman, P., Compton, C., Igra, D., Ronfeldt, M., Shahan, E., & Williamson, P. W. (2009). Teaching practice: A cross-professional perspective. *Teachers College Record, 111*, 2055–2100.

Grossman, P., Hammerness, K., & McDonald, M. (2009). Redefining teacher: Re-imagining teacher education. *Teachers and Teaching: Theory and Practice, 15*(2), 273–290.

Grossman, P., & McDonald, M. (2008). Back to the future: Directions for research in teaching and teacher education. *American Educational Research Journal, 45*(1), 184–205.

Grossman, P., & Shahan, E. (2005, April). *The anatomy of practice: The use of decomposition.* Paper presented at the annual meeting of the American Educational Research Association, Montreal, Canada.

Hattie, J., & Timperley H. (2007). The power of feedback. *Review of Educational Research, 77*(1), 81–112.

Hiebert, J., Gallimore, R., & Stigler, J. W. (2002). A knowledge base for the teaching profession: What would it look like and how can we get one? *Educational Researcher, 31*(5), 3–15.

Hiebert, J., Morris, A., Berk, D., & Jansen, A. (2007). Preparing teachers to learn from teaching. *Journal of Teacher Education, 58*, 47–61.

Kazemi, E., & Hintz, A. (2008). *Fostering productive mathematical discussions in the classroom.* Unpublished manuscript. Seattle, WA: University of Washington.

Kazemi, E., Lampert, M., & Ghousseini, H. (2007). *Conceptualizing and using routines of practice in mathematics teaching to advance professional education.* Report to the Spencer Foundation, Chicago, IL.

Klausmeier, H. J. (1974). *Conceptual learning and development: A cognitive view.* New York, NY: Academic Press.

Klenowski, V. (1995). Student self-evaluation process in student-centered teaching and learning contexts of Australia and England. *Assessment in Education, 2*, 145–163.

Krechevsky, M. (2012). Changing our skin: Creating collective knowledge in American classrooms, *The New Educator, 8*(1), 12–37.

Kucan, L., & Palincsar, A. (with Busse, T., Heisey, N., Klingelhofer, R., Rimbey, M., & Schutz, K.). (2010, April). *Text-based discussion: The case of reading.* Paper presented at the annual meeting of the American Educational Research Association, Denver, CO.

Lampert, M. (1985). How do teachers manage to teach? Perspectives on problems in practice. *Harvard Educational Review, 55*(2), 178–194.

Lampert, M. (2001). *Teaching problems and the problems of teaching.* New Haven, CT: Yale University Press.

Lampert, M., & Ball, D. L. (1998). *Mathematics, teaching and multimedia: Investigations of real practice.* New York, NY: Teachers College Press.

Lampert, M., & Graziani, F. (2009). Instructional activities as a tool for teachers' and teacher educators' learning. *The Elementary School Journal, 109*(5), 491–509.

Larrivee, B. (2000). Transforming teaching practice: Becoming the critically reflective teacher. *Reflective Practice, 1*(3), 293–307.

Leinhardt, G. (1989). Math lessons: A contrast of novice and expert competence. *Journal for Research in Mathematics Education, 20*(1), 52–75.

Leinhardt, G. (2004). Instructional explanations: A commonplace for teaching and a location for contrast. In V. Richardson (Ed.), *Handbook of research on teaching* (4th ed.; pp. 333–357). Washington, DC: American Educational Research Association.

Levine, A. (2006). *Educating school teachers.* Washington, DC: The Education Schools Project.

Marzano, R., Pickering, D., & Pollock, J. (2001). *Classroom instruction that works.* Alexandria, VA: ASCD.

McArdle, F. (2010). Preparing quality teachers: Making learning visible. *Australian Journal of Teacher Education, 35*(8), 60–78.

McDonald, J., Mohr, N., Dichter, A., & McDonald, E. (2013). *The power of protocols: An educator's guide to better practice.* New York, NY: Teachers College Press.

Meyer, J., Land, R. & Baillie, C. (2010). *Threshold concepts and transformational learning.* Rotterdam: Sense Publishers.

Mezirow, J. (1990). *Fostering critical reflection in adulthood.* San Francisco, CA: Jossey-Bass.

Montgomery, K. (2001). *Authentic assessment: A guide for elementary teachers.* New York, NY: Longman.

Moskal, B. M. (2000). Scoring rubrics: What, when, and how? *Practical Assessment, Research, & Evaluation, 7*(3). Retrieved from PAREonline.net/getvn.asp?v=7&n=3

Moss, P. A. (2011). Analyzing the teaching of professional practice. *Teachers College Record, 113*(12), 2878–2896.

Namubiru, P. S. (2007). *The theory-practice discourse in initial teacher education: Perspectives, problems, prospects.* Bayreuth, Germany: Breitinger.

Nitko, A. J. (2001). *Educational assessment of students* (3rd ed.). Upper Saddle River, NJ: Merrill.

Noddings, N. (2003). Is teaching a practice? *Journal of Philosophy of Education, 37*(2), 241–251.

Orsmond, P., Merry, S., & Reiling, K. (2013). Moving feedback forward: Theory to practice. *Assessment and Evaluation in Higher Education, 38*(2), 240–252.

Paul, R., & Elder, L. (2006). *The thinker's guide to how to read a paragraph: The art of close reading.* Dillon Beach, CA: The Foundation for Critical Thinking.

Perkins, D. N., & Ritchhart, R. (2004). When is good thinking? In D. Y. Dai & R. J. Sternberg (Eds.), *Motivation, emotion, and cognition: Integrative perspectives on intellectual functioning and development* (pp. 351–384). Mahwah, NJ: Erlbaum.

Perkins, D. N., & Salomon, G. (1992). *Transfer of learning: Contribution to the International Encyclopedia of Education* (2nd ed.). Oxford: Pergamon Press.

Peters, C. W., & Kenney, P. A. (2003, January). *The road less traveled by: Characteristics of alternative teacher certification programs at the graduate level.* Paper presented at the annual meeting of the American Association of Colleges of Teacher Education, New Orleans, LA.

Peters, C. W., & Kenney, P. A. (2004, February). *Designing, implementing, and evaluating a master's degree with certification program.* Paper presented at the annual meeting of the American Association of Colleges of Teacher Education, Chicago, IL.

Peters, C. W., Wixson, K. K., Valencia, S. W., & Pearson, P. D. (1993). Changing statewide reading assessment: A case study of Michigan and Illinois. In B. R. Gifford (Ed.), *Policy perspectives on educational testing* (pp. 295–391). Boston, MA: Kluwer Academic Publishers.

Putnam, R., & Borko, H. (1997). Teacher learning: Implications of new views of cognition. In B. J. Biddle, T. L. Good, & I. F. Goodson (Eds.), *International handbook of teachers and teaching* (vol. 2; pp. 1223–1296). Dordrecht, Netherlands: Kluwer.

Rich, M. (2014, April 26). Obama administration plans rules to grade teacher preparation programs. *New York Times*, p. A12.

Richmond, G., Juzwik, M. M., & Steele, M. D. (2012). Trajectories of teacher identity development across institutional contexts: Constructing a narrative approach. *Teachers College Record, 113*(9), 1863–1905.

Ritchhart, R. (2004). *Intellectual character: What it is, why it matters, and how to get it.* San Francisco, CA: Jossey-Bass.

Ritchhart, R. (2015). *Creating cultures of thinking: The eight forces we must master to truly transform our schools.* San Francisco: Jossey-Bass.

Ritchhart, R., & Perkins, D. (2008). Teaching students to think. *Educational Leadership, 6*(5), 57–61.

Rowan, B., Correnti, R., & Miller, R. (2002). What large-scale, survey research tells us about teacher effects on student achievement: Insights from the Prospects study of elementary schools. *Teachers College Record, 104*(8), 1525–1567.

Salomon, G., & Perkins, D. (1988, September). Teaching for transfer. *Educational Leadership*, 22–32.

Samson, G. E., Strykowski, B., Weinstein, T., & Walberg, H. J. (1987). The effects of teacher questioning levels on student achievement. *Journal of Educational Research, 80*, 290–295.

Sanders, W. L., & Rivers, J. C. (1996). *Cumulative and residual effects of teachers on future student academic achievement.* Knoxville, TN: University of Tennessee.

Schön, D. (1987). *Educating the reflective practitioner: Toward a new design for teaching and learning in the professions.* San Francisco, CA: Jossey-Bass.

Shanker, A. (1996). Quality assurance: What must be done to strengthen the teaching profession. *Phi Delta Kappan, 78*(3), 220–224.

Shepard, L. A. (1997). *Measuring achievement: What does it mean to test for robust understanding?* Princeton, NJ: Policy Information Center, Educational Testing Service.

Shepard, L. A. (2000). The role of assessment in a learning culture. *Educational Researcher, 29*(7), 4–14.

Sherin, M. G. (2004). New perspectives on the role of video in teacher education. In J. Brophy (Ed.), *Using video in teacher education: Advances in research on teaching* (vol. 10; pp. 1–27). Oxford, England: Elsevier.

Shulman, L. S. (1986). Those who understand: Knowledge growth in teaching. *Educational Researcher, 15*(2), 4–14.

Shulman, L. S. (1987). Knowledge and teaching: Foundations of the new reform. *Harvard Educational Review, 57*(1), 1–22.

Sleep, L., Boerst, T., & Ball, D. L. (2007, March). *Learning to do the work of teaching in a practice-based methods course.* Paper presented at the research pre-session of the National Council of Teachers of Mathematics, Atlanta, GA.

Smith, E. (2011). Teaching critical reflection. *Teaching in Higher Education, 16*(2), 211–223.

Stanford University Teacher Education Program. (2002–2003). *Stanford Teacher Education Handbook.* Palo Alto, CA: Author.

Stanton, T. K. (1990). Liberal arts, experiential learning and public service: Necessary ingredients for socially responsible undergraduate education. In J. Kendall & Associates (Eds.), *Combining service and learning* (vol. I; pp. 175–189). Raleigh, NC: National Society for Internships and Experiential Education.

Stiggins, R. J. (1987). Design and development of performance assessments. *Educational Measurement: Issues and Practices, 6*(3), 33–42.

Stiggins, R. J. (1994). *Student-centered classroom assessment.* New York, NY: Macmillan.

Stigler, J. W., & Hiebert, J. (1997). Understanding and improving classroom mathematics instruction: An overview of the TIMSS video study. *Phi Delta Kappan, 79*(1), 14–21.

Suarez, S. C. (2006). Making learning visible through documentation: Creating a culture of inquiry among pre-service teachers. *The New Educator, 2*(1), 33–55.

Teacher Education Initiative Curriculum Group. (2008). *High leverage teaching practices.* Unpublished working paper. University of Michigan School of Education, Ann Arbor.

Teaching Works. (2014). High leverage practice. University of Michigan: School of Education, Ann Arbor, MI. Retrieved from teachingworks.org/work-of-teaching/high-leverage-practices

Thompson, S., & Thompson, N. (2008). *The critically reflective practitioner.* Basingstoke, England & New York, NY: Palgrave Macmillan.

Tombari, M., & Borich, G. (1999). *Authentic assessment in classroom: Applications and practice.* Upper Saddle River, NJ: Merrill.

Trice, A. D. (2000). *A handbook of classroom assessment.* New York, NY: Longman.

U.S. News & World Report. (2014). Best grad schools 2015: Schools of education. Retrieved from grad-schools.usnews.rankingsandreviews.com/best-graduate-schools/top-education-schools/secondary-teacher-education-rankings?int=9a2b08

Vacca, R. & Vacca, J. A. (2002). *Content area reading: Literacy and learning across the curriculum* (7th ed.). Boston, MA: Allyn & Bacon.

Vacca, R., & Vacca, J. A. (2008). *Content area reading: Literacy and learning across the curriculum* (9th ed.). Boston, MA: Allyn & Bacon.

van Woerkom, M. (2010). Critical reflection as a rationalistic ideal. *Adult Education Quarterly, 60*(4), 339–356.

Wehlage, G. G., Newmann, F. M., & Secada, W. A. (1996). Standards for authentic achievement and pedagogy. In F. M. Newmann & Associates (Eds.), *Authentic achievement: Restructuring schools for intellectual quality* (pp. 21–48). San Francisco, CA: Jossey-Bass.

Wiggins, G. (1992). Creating tests worth taking. *Educational Leadership, 49*, 26–33.

Wiggins, G., & McTighe, J. (1998). *Understanding by design.* Alexandria, VA: Association for Supervision and Curriculum Development.

Wiggins, G., & McTighe, J. (2005). *Understanding by design* (2nd ed.). Alexandria, VA: Association for Supervision and Curriculum Development.

Will, G. (2006, January 16). Ed schools vs. education. *Newsweek*, p. 98.

Wixson, K., & Peters, C. W. (1987). Comprehension assessment: Implementing an interactive view of reading. *Educational Psychologist, 22*, 333–356.

Zeichner, K. (2006). Reflections of a university-based teacher educator on the future of college and university-based teacher education. *Journal of Teacher Education, 57*(3), 326–340.

Index

About the Authors

Charles W. Peters is a former professor of educational practice at the University of Michigan. He coordinated and taught in the Secondary Master's of Arts and Certification Program (MAC). Before coming to the University of Michigan, he was a secondary content literacy consultant for Oakland Schools, a regional educational support agency in Michigan. His scholarly focus is on secondary literacy and assessment. Dr. Peters has edited two books, written numerous chapters for other books, and published many articles in such periodicals as the *Reading Research Quarterly, The Educational Psychologist, Educational Leadership, Language Arts, The Journal of Reading,* and *The Reading Teacher.* He has also served on numerous state and national committees and been a consultant on many national and state projects. Some of these include various state curricular framework and assessment committees, a variety of committees for the National Assessment of Educational Progress, The College Board, National Assessment Governing Board, New Standards Project, Achieve, the American Institutes for Research, and the Council of Chief State School Officers.

Deanna Birdyshaw is currently on the faculty of the University of Michigan Teacher Education Program. Her undergraduate and graduate courses focus on literacy in the content areas and video analysis of classroom practices to improve secondary teacher preparation. Dr. Birdyshaw served for 2 years as the University of Michigan's coordinator of secondary teacher education and currently cochairs the International Literacy Association Task Force on Teacher Preparation for Literacy Instruction. Dr. Birdyshaw also served as associate director of the Center for the Improvement of Early Reading Achievement (CIERA) from 1999 to 2005. In addition to her work at the University of Michigan, Dr. Birdyshaw served as English language arts consultant for the state of Michigan and taught English and literacy to secondary students. Dr. Birdyshaw's areas of research include the development of preservice teachers, disciplinary literacy, and schoolwide assessment systems.

Amy Bacevich is clinical faculty lecturer at Northern Kentucky University. She supervises student teachers and teaches courses in the undergraduate elementary teacher education program. Her work addresses redesigning teacher education curriculum to focus on the study and practice of teaching. She works on developing and using methods, including video study, written cases, and field-based coaching, that support novices' development as teachers. She has presented at conferences and at teacher education programs on clinical practice design issues, including the use of alternative settings, field-based instructional activities for teacher education, and the use of video technology to support novice teacher learning. Dr. Bacevich is a former elementary school teacher.